Date Due

LAYMAN'S CHURCH

LAYMAN'S CHURCH

by

J. A. T. ROBINSON (Bishop of Woolwich)
DOUGLAS RHYMES   LESLIE PAUL
PETER WHITELEY   MICHAEL BRUCE
MARK GIBBS   HAROLD WILSON

with an Introduction by
TIMOTHY BEAUMONT

LONDON
LUTTERWORTH PRESS

First published 1963

Second Impression 1963

COPYRIGHT © 1963 LUTTERWORTH PRESS

4 BOUVERIE STREET

LONDON E.C.4

Printed in Great Britain
by Page Bros. (Norwich) Ltd., Norwich

Contents

Introduction

THE MINISTRY CONFERENCE group from which this book comes was founded during a residential conference at Keble College, Oxford, in the summer of 1960 and soon came to be known as the Keble Group.

The conference under the chairmanship of the Right Reverend John Robinson, Bishop of Woolwich, stemmed in its turn from a statement on Parochial Reform coming from the younger clergy of the Birmingham Diocese. The conference was well and enthusiastically attended and as a result a continuation committee was formed with myself as Secretary to issue a quarterly news-letter and to organize the way forward.

It soon became clear that any scheme for parochial reform or rethinking the task of ministry which did not enlist the laity as equal partners was wrong in theory and useless in practice. We therefore organized a week-end lay conference in London in the winter of 1962 and the papers in this book are the main speeches at that conference.

With the exception of the opening address, we asked both a layman and a priest to speak on each subject; apart from the speakers only laymen were present and the discussion on each topic was long and lively.

We offer these papers not only as a contribution to the thinking of the Anglican Church but also as an earnest of our determination to catch up with other churches which we encounter in the Ecumenical field in the realization of the proper place of the laity in the Church.

TIMOTHY BEAUMONT

1

THE MINISTRY AND THE LAITY

by

THE BISHOP OF WOOLWICH

IT IS WORTH starting from the connotation of the title. I take it that my subject is intended to be the ministry *of* the laity. But undoubtedly to the average Englishman—indeed to the average Churchman—the title would signify almost the exact opposite, for going into the ministry means ceasing to be a layman. "The Ministry *and* the Laity" would therefore be taken to be simply another way of saying "The Clergy and the Laity".

This brings one straight up against the deeply ingrained assumption that runs through almost all our thinking until we are pulled up and told otherwise, that the ministry is the prerogative of the clergy. I noted this typical error in my review for *The Observer* of Paul Ferris's otherwise salutary and stimulating examination of the Church of England. He equated throughout, not merely "going into the ministry", but "going into the Church", with "being ordained". I said that I thought it was a legitimate criticism of his book that the whole dimension of the laity and its ministry virtually received no place. Subsequently, I received a letter from a Presbyterian minister in Liverpool, from which I would like to quote a paragraph.

"You charge Ferris, I imagine rightly, with omitting the entire dimension of the holy common people of God, and with seeing the priest not as an integral member of a transforming

fellowship, but always isolated, whether in holiness or hopeless-
ness. Further, none of the bishops is depicted as father in God to
his people. Yet this is, with notable exceptions, just the impression
that the sympathetic non-Anglican does get as he looks in from
the outside, rubs shoulders in hospital corridors, and talks and
listens at ecumenical meetings. The average Anglican incumbent
is, perhaps unwittingly, clerically minded. I was talking some
time back with my own local vicar, who would certainly appear
on the credit side on any list of Ferris's. We came to discuss the
eldership and the pastoral function of the sessions. His reaction
was very strong. He felt himself quite unable to demit his pastoral
responsibility in any degree, and said that he could not allow any
layman to intrude into what he regarded as a sacred sphere into
which he was ordained to function."

I had to admit in replying that I feared that this was only too
fair a comment, and probably went for ninety per cent of the
clergy of the Church of England. But equally, I think, it's only
fair to say that it doesn't go only for ninety per cent of the clergy.
It probably goes for ninety-nine per cent of the laity. I heard
John Lawrence, the editor of *Frontier*, the other day give this
analysis: "What does the layman really want? He wants a
building which looks like a church; a clergyman dressed in the
way he approves; services of the kind he's been used to, *and to be
left alone*." I think that is a pretty fair summary of what the average layman demands of the Church of England. And as Bishop
Barry of Southwell put it in his book, *Asking The Right Questions*,
the nominal C. of E. man is still on the Latin side of the Reforma-
tion watershed. He believes that religion is the business of the
parson.

Nothing, indeed, is more deeply entrenched in our society
than what I have called this "clergy line". In fact, it is virtually
impossible for us to imagine a church without this division
between clergy on the one hand and laity on the other. Yet, of
course, it was not a primitive division in the Church, and indeed,
as Bishop Barry shows in the same book, it is fundamentally an
alien importation. The early Church knew, of course, a very

great diversity of ministries within the Body. It did not suffer from the impoverishment and standardization of ministries which we know. There was every conceivable contribution of ministry and liturgy to the life of the early Church—from each man according to his ability. And yet, there is no evidence that at any one point within this diversity a line was drawn above which, as it were, came those with dog-collar status and below which came "the laity". This line is drawn at different places in our different traditions. In the Church of England it is very clearly drawn below the diaconate, though in practice the functions of a deacon and of a reader are far closer together than the functions of a deacon and a priest. Moreover, at certain points there is confusion amounting almost to dishonesty. Are, for instance, deaconesses above or below the clergy line? They are certainly said to be ordained; on the other hand, they are apparently not in holy orders.

But the point I want to make relates not to the confusion but to the fact that this line was introduced into the Church almost entirely under secular influence. It was taken over from the patterns of civic life and it became entrenched at the time of the Peace of the Church under Constantine, when certain privileges and benefits were extended to the clergy of the Christian Church, which had previously been bestowed by the Roman Empire on the heathen priesthood. And at that point, of course, it became important to define who was entitled to these benefits and who was not. Hence the beginning of a legal division between members of "the clergy" and "the laity". This gradually became more firmly established until in the twelfth century the lawyer Gratian could state quite categorically, "There are two sorts of Christians", by which he didn't mean good Christians and bad Christians, but clergy and laity. Hence too, the development from which we are still suffering, of the *ecclesia docens*—the teaching church—on the one hand, and the *ecclesia discens*—the learning church—on the other.

This division has, of course, subsequently been buttressed by every sort of argument, sociological, psychological and theological. Still the clergy line affords a powerful status symbol, which becomes psychologically the more important as the real status diminishes and the parson's role in society becomes more and more uncertain. We may not often hear the phrase these days, "Respect for the cloth", but this is something which, I suspect, is still deeply ingrained in the average Englishman's reaction to the clergy, whether positively or negatively. And it is still something which, deep down, the average clergyman expects of the laity, and which he insists shall in some way or other be compensated for if it is not given in the old-fashioned way.

Clergy are still, in our Church, people who come, as it were, from the other side of the fence. They are men sent, if not from God, at any rate from the bishop or the patron: they are men who arrive in the parish, who are placed there from above or from without by some mysterious processes in which the power of the laity is merely to advise (possibly) and consent (certainly). And the whole way in which we train our clergy reinforces this. The very language of "selection conferences" implies that we cream off an élite, whom we then put into seminaries, shut up by themselves, train out of any relation to the people to whom they are going to minister, and, in due course, release upon a receptive church.

The clergy are those within the Church who are given the "know-how", which it is their job to dispense in various degrees of dilution to the rest of the Body. And our society, if it has lost respect for authority, still has respect for the specialist. Many of the clergy, I think, tend to boost their morale by the feeling that they at any rate have the "gen". My children, when I go out, as I constantly do, and leave them at home, ask, "Oh, Daddy, are you going to tell the people things?" And that, I am sure, is a very fair description of how very many clergymen think of lay training.

Then, of course, this line is further entrenched, and very powerfully entrenched in our established church, by the law. The parson's freehold provides, once again, a powerful status symbol, and that fantastic procedure that takes place, I imagine still, at the beginning of most induction services, by which the first act of the parson is to lock his laity out of the church, is a vivid expression of this entire understanding of the matter.

It is also reinforced by our whole ecclesiastical ethos. This is most patently so in the papalist tradition, where there is a kind of mystique, a divinity, which hedges a priest, who is regarded in some sense as a higher species of humanity than the layman. But we all in our different traditions have our ways of expressing this difference. In the Church of England it is more like membership of an exclusive clerical club, called Crockfords. In the Reformed Churches there is the build-up of "the preacher" in his black gown, who stands six feet above contradiction delivering the message of God to the rest of His waiting people. (I once heard a German Lutheran say, "The trouble is that God is like the minister: we don't see him during the week, and we don't understand him on Sundays.") And this is true of traditions which on the face of it would appear most lay-dominated. The Methodists are often quoted as the church in which the layman has most opportunities for ministry. But you have only to read Ted Wickham's *Church and People in an Industrial City*[1] to see that in nineteenth-century Sheffield, at any rate, the Methodist was the most clericalized church of them all. How it survived is almost a greater miracle than how the Church of England survived!

But the last and most powerful line of defence in this perimeter within which the clergy live is, of course, theology. The clergyman is seen from the theological point of view as having the power to do what the others cannot do—and at this point no-one can touch him. Like the priesthood of the Old Testament, he mediates between the people and God. Religion is still his preserve, and the Sacraments at any rate are firmly in his hands. And this is not merely as a result of clerical pretensions. It is also, I think, something which is deeply rooted in the layman's consciousness. I remember when I was chaplain at Wells Theological College how I used to go round the Somerset villages doing locum work. When one went to Mattins or Evensong

[1] Lutterworth Press, 1957.

everything was fine. Everyone knew exactly what to do. You merely had to come in, take the service, and all the rest was looked after. But if you went to take a Holy Communion service, no-one knew anything at all. In the absence of the vicar nothing was available. I once had to begin by looking for the key of the safe in his cassock pocket. Not even the churchwardens seemed to take any responsibility for this service. It was the preserve of the clergy, and this was apparently the way everyone was content to have it.

It is at this theological point, at the heart of the matter, that I am convinced we have got to begin if we are going to try to reform the whole system. For unhappily, or perhaps happily, it simply will not stand up to a truly biblical doctrine of the Church. In the Old Testament, indeed, the priesthood was vicarious in the sense that the priest did on behalf of the people what they could not do: there was one tribe in Irsael which was priestly, and eleven that were not. But in the New Testament this kind of division is utterly abolished. There is one mediator between God and man, the High Priest, Christ Jesus, and no priestly caste within the Body. The entire Body is a royal priesthood, and every member has his share in that priesthood by virtue of his baptism. The ordained ministry, within this covenant, is not a vicarious one, but a representative one. It is commissioned and set apart to exercise in the name of the Body, Head and members alike, the ministry which belongs to the whole. What is given to the ordained minister is formal authority to preach and proclaim in the name of the whole Church what every member has not only the right but the duty to proclaim. He is given formal authority to exercise the ministry of reconciliation and forgiveness which belongs by right to every member of the healing community. He is given formal authority to lead and preside at the celebration which is the con-celebration of the whole people of God. For in this sense every celebration is a lay celebration. The celebrant is the entire laos, of which the bishop or presbyter is "the president". (The early Church never used the term "the celebrant" as we do, of an individual.)

In other words, if we ask what was distinctive about the ordained ministry, I don't think we get the deepest or the truest answer in terms of what the others cannot do. There are, indeed, things which by the Church's own discipline and order its ordained ministry is given authority to do in its name. But of course these things vary. Confirmation, for instance, is an obvious example where different communions in different ages have varied greatly in the amount of delegation they have been prepared to permit. In any case, all these particular functions are what the Church itself sets its clergy apart to perform in its name. For the ministry which they exercise is always the ministry of the whole Body—not, of course, the ministry of the Body apart from the Head, as if their authority came simply from below, but neither of the Head apart from the Body, but of the Head working through the Body. Theirs is a representative ministry of and to the whole people of God.

And it is precisely because it is so representative that it occupies such a key position and crucial responsibility. For in practice the level of ministry in a local church will seldom rise above the level of the ordained minister. And that is why the quality of our ordained ministry is infinitely more important than its quantity.

We hear a great deal about shortage of clergy, and nobody needs to speak to me about that, or to convince me of it. The whole time one sees opportunities simply going to pot, churches merely ticking over when they could break through if only there was more manpower available. But, I constantly wonder, and I wonder more the longer I go on in this job, whether we do not, in fact, ordain too many people. I am sure we baptize too many people: I am pretty certain I confirm too many people: and I suspect that we ordain too many people. I am more and more convinced that bad priests are worse than no priests. For the ordained ministry is, as it were, the channel—or the bottleneck— of the ministry of Christ to His people, and through them to the world. And what the Church does to a man at ordination is to say: "You are to be that channel—or that bottleneck." When the channels get blocked or furred up, the Spirit, thank God, does find other ways through. But we neglect these channels at our peril.

In this connection, it is, I think, vitally important that the structure and the organization of our church should not be such as to allow every ordained man within about seven years of his ordination thereafter to become a permanent thermostat to his congregation, so that the temperature of a church can never rise above his own spiritual, moral, or intellectual temperature. There are countless clergy who have a real ministry to perform, but whose gifts of imagination, to speak of nothing elese, are such that they should never be permitted to be in a position in which they can thus hold down the temperature of a local church for the rest of their ministry. It is not, on the whole, that they can't be turned out. (Most of the clergy one would like to turn out would be only too willing to go, if only one could conscientiously put them somewhere else.) It is that they are in a position to say: "I am king of my castle—you dare step one yard over my parish boundary." The trouble is that no-one *else* can do anything in that parish if they don't.

It is ironical that in this essay on the ministry of the laity, I have spent almost all my time so far on the clergy. But it has, I think, been necessary. This is partly because I do want to stress that I have, and I believe our church has, a high doctrine of the ordained ministry, and that nothing is gained whatever by having a high doctrine of the laity at the expense of a low doctrine of the ordained priesthood. But I have mainly concentrated on this because I believe this clergy line, and what we do about it, is absolutely crucial to the release of any genuine ministry of the laity. Moreover, our *theological* judgments at this point are the most crucial thing of all, because if we understand the ordained man as exercising a vicarious ministry, as opposed to a representative ministry, then every concession made to the laity will inevitably be and appear to be at the expense of the clergy. And this, I believe, underlies the lack of trust of the laity, which bedevils the largely well-meaning attitude of the majority of our clergy. They fear that if the laity are really given their head, then their own place and ministry in the Church will be correspondingly diminished.

If, on the other hand, we see the ordained ministry as truly representative of the ministry of the whole Body, then there is, I believe, no such tension. One expands automatically with the expansion of the other; and indeed there is for the clergy, as many of them are now finding, a tremendous increase and release of their ministry, as they discover themselves for the first time as the servants of the servants of God. And this conception of the ministry, which is after all the papal conception of the ministry (for it is the proud title of the Pope that he is the *servus servorum dei*) is, I believe, the clue to the whole revolution. For we can never hold too high a doctrine of the ordained ministry if we really see it, as the New Testament does, as the ministry of the servant, in direct extension of the ministry of the Son of Man who came not to be ministered unto but to minister.

But it is essential that we do see it this way round—that the clergy are *the servants* of the laity. As Hans Rudi Weber has put it: "The laity are not helpers of the clergy so that the clergy can do their job, but the clergy are helpers of the whole people of God, so that the laity can be the Church." And I suppose in theory all of us would readily subscribe to that sentiment. But it is almost completely reversed in so many of our practices. And most blatantly is it so reversed in the service by which every priest of the Church of England is instituted to his cure of souls. In the course of the induction service the congregation is asked: "Will you pray continually for this your minister who is set over you in the Lord, and help him forward in all the duties of his holy calling?" It is the vicar's responsibility to do all these things: it is the people's responsibility to help him. "This is apparently the picture of the parish in action which the Anglican Church wishes to emphasize and perpetuate: a struggling vicar grappling with an impossible task, visiting, organizing, evangelizing, preaching, praying, teaching, celebrating, while his churchwardens, and those of the faithful who can be persuaded, *help him*." These words are taken from an article by Andrew Hake, which appeared in *Prism*, April 1962, entitled: "So I tore up the Printed Form of Service." But I need not expand his point, which is that at the moment all over the Anglican Communion, in one form or another, a perverted doctrine of the Church and its ministry is being proclaimed every time a new vicar is inducted.

A truer doctrine of the priesthood of the laity, or rather of the *Laos*, is, thank God, being recovered in our day. But this conception must also, I think, be balanced equally firmly on the other side by what the report *Gender and Ministry*, presented recently to the Church Assembly, called "the laity of the priesthood". The whole Church, ordained and unordained alike, is called to be a lay body. By this of course I do not mean (as the Quakers would interpret it) that it is not to have its sacramental ministers, but that it is essentially and always a body which is immersed in the world.

And this, I believe, provides a right starting point for a true definition of the laity. To define the laity in opposition to the clergy is itself a by-product of clericalism. The designation that for me goes nearer to the heart of the matter than any other is that given in pages 17–22 of Father Yves Congar's great book *Lay People in the Church*.[1] The layman, he says, is one for whom the things of this world really exist for their own sake: their truth is not, as it were, swallowed up and destroyed by a higher reference, so that everything has first to become religious in order to be interesting, and the secular is important and relevant only if it can somehow be turned to the service of the Church or violently baptized into Christ. And this temper of mind, what Congar calls "a genuine laicity", need not, and must not, be confined to those not ordained. It is a temper which should characterize the entire Church. It is what Dietrich Bonhoeffer was pleading for in his call for an authentic Christian worldliness.

I believe that this is, in practice, something we have got to insist upon time and time again. Perhaps I could illustrate this by reference back to the sort of thing that I constantly encountered

[1] Bloomsbury Publishing Co., 1957.

while I was in Cambridge when dealing with a body which many of you will know, and which I refer to with great respect —the Cambridge Inter-Collegiate Christian Union. Now of no body in the Church could it be claimed that it was less priest-ridden. It was essentially a "lay" body with a deep suspicion of priestcraft. And yet my constant charge against this body was that it never really understood what it meant to train a person as a layman. It never saw a vocation to the secular as something which a man could have, as it were, for its own sake and in its own right. The best that could be said of the world was that it might be used and turned into occasions of evangelism, and the only reason why a person would take a secular job was that in this job the Lord might use him for pulling out a few brands from the burning. And, of course, seen like that a secular job was essentially a second best. If you were a hundred-percenter you wanted to be in full-time evangelism. You didn't want to spend a lot of your day turning nuts: you were much better employed saving souls. And constantly, therefore, one found that when a person was converted by the C.I.C.C.U. it was only a matter of time before he came along and said: "I think the Lord is calling me to be ordained." For this was virtually the only way in which he could be an all-out Christian seen in terms of that sort of theology.

Furthermore, this conception of the genuine laity of the priest-hood is an important corrective to our current stress on the priesthood of the laity, if we are not to think of the laity in purely Church-centred terms.

In a recent number of *Frontier*, Mark Gibbs wrote an admirable article called "Two Kinds of Laity", which he distinguished as follows: the first, which for convenience we may label Type A, have their main interests in the world outside the Church; in their careers, in trade, in university teaching, in local or national politics, in different voluntary organizations like Rotary, or some social welfare association, and above all in their home and family life. This means that their way of serving God will also be in these worldly preoccupations.

Laity Type B, who are a small percentage of the whole Church of God, almost as small as the clergy in comparison with the great mass of world-centred people, are those who, to the amazement and reluctant admiration of their fellow laymen, actually have their main interest in life centred on their church and its organization: who are keen lay preachers, Sunday School teachers, fund-raisers, church councillors and the like.

This, I believe, is an important distinction, or difference of emphasis, and we have to begin, I think, by recognizing that almost all the people we ever talk to in any kind of lay training tend to be Laity Type B. They belong to a very small minority. But these are the tame laity, the laity that we can always round up, men and women who are to some extent already in the organization of the Church. They are no worse for that—at least not on the whole. But it is going to be fearfully easy, in the kind of break-through which I very much hope we shall see in this matter of lay training, to concentrate quite disproportionately on this second, and relatively small, group. For it is so tempting to see the revival of lay ministry simply in terms of waking the sleeping partners of the clergy and making them better members of the organization church.

At this point I think we can take a warning from what has happened in the United States. For there, on the one hand, they use the laity far better than we have ever got round to doing in this country. One sees a lay participation in the whole life of the Church, which at first sight makes one tremendously envious. On the other hand, they have gone to town on the organization church in a way that almost passes belief. And if you want a devastating diagnosis of the American religious establishment, I commend to you a book which has just come to me from across the Atlantic called *The Noise of Solemn Assemblies*, by Peter Berger.[1] He is a lay sociologist who has done a sort of Vance Packard on the American church, but done it, not from the side-lines, but very much from the angle of the committed layman. He sees the picture as, in many ways, so appalling, that he

[1] Doubledays, 1961.

seriously proposes the thesis, which bears much thinking about, that participation in organized religion is *a* Christian vocation. The Church, as represented in the churches, may have got to such a point that it is a serious question for the layman whether he can really exercise his discipleship primarily within the religious organization or not. And this same question is also raised by Alec Vidler's penetrating contribution, "Religion and the National Church", in the symposium he edited called *Soundings*.[1]

Inevitably there will always be within the life of the Church two poles: one which is primarily church-centred, parish-centred, the other which is world-centred. (This applies not merely to the layman but also to the man in orders; and if we had more ordained men who were not parish-centred but world-centred, I believe the balance would be better restored.) But here, both for the ordained and unordained, there is a genuine difference of vocation, and we should not be tempted into thinking that either is more authentic than the other. For I detect the emergence of a new status symbol in the Church, which goes under the battle cry: "Worldlier than thou." And biblically speaking this is just as much a danger, though not yet such a big danger, as "Holier than thou." For ultimately the Christian is neither church-centred nor world-centred, but Kingdom-centred. For the Church is the instrument of God for reducing the world to the Kingdom, and the ministry of the laity is the ministry of God *both* within the structures of the Church *and* within the structures of the world.

St. Paul uses in Romans 13:6 a most striking phrase of the secular authorities. He says they are *leitourgoi theou*—liturgical ministers of God. And this, I think, is an important emphasis if we are to get our doctrine of the ministry of the laity right. For it involves us in as high a doctrine of the State as it does of the Church, and implies that Christians must be equally involved in the ministry of each. This is perhaps a point that needs stressing, because I don't think it is usually made. Even those who concentrate most on the world-centredness of the Church do not

[1] Cambridge University Press, 1962.

really bring it out. Hendrik Kraemer, for instance, in his book *A Theology of the Laity*,[1] stresses all the way through that the ministry is always the ministry *of* the Church *to* the world. But the New Testament speaks of a ministry of God which is not "of" the Church, and which need not, therefore, be exercised by committed Christians. It would be truer to say that some are called to the ministry of the Kingdom (or better perhaps the ministry of the King) through the structures of the Church, and some are called to the ministry of the Kingdom through the structures of the world. It is these latter who seem to me most in need of the help of the Church (whether they are Christians or not)—and who least get it.

[1] Lutterworth Press, 1958.

2

THE PLACE OF THE LAITY IN THE PARISH (i)

by

DOUGLAS RHYMES

THE BISHOP OF WOOLWICH has shown us what is the nature of the ministry of the laity and its connection with that of the ordained laity who are the clergy, but the important thing to remember in all this is that there is only one ministry—the ministry of the laos, the people of God—and that the New Testament knew no distinction between what we call the clergy and what we call the laity save a distinction of function. Bishop Lightfoot wrote some eighty years ago: "All Christians are God's laity and all are God's clergy." When I was a layman, as I was for some time before becoming a priest, I had precisely the same tasks as I have now, but I did not recognize it so well because, in common with all other laity, I was taught to regard myself as simply the passive recipient of the teaching and direction of the clergy; I was meant to help the clergy. I therefore accepted the position of the spiritually illiterate, the led rather than the leader, and the spiritually immature both in thinking and in the relation of the thinking to the world. It would never have entered my head to think of initiating any activity within the parish—that was the function of the clergy.

We now, however, are beginning to recognize that in the work of the Church the function of leadership does not and should not rest with the clergy; that the laity, not the clergy, are the spearhead of the evangelism which is to be done; that the clergy must now be content to help the laity to be the Church, and to act as the source-material of the laity in matters theological and as the functionaries of sacrament and the shepherds of pastoral care. This is only very slowly dawning upon the clergy, however, and is in many quarters actively resented (as we are finding in our lay training at Wychcroft); and there are many laity who will have to fight hard if they are to exercise a role which is not just subservient to the wishes and plans of the clergy. As an example of this I would mention a letter I received recently from one of the clergy, and a very good one, in the diocese in which I serve. He wrote of the plans he was making for the further study of those who had been here on a Lay Training Conference; but never once did it occur to him to take those who had been here into his confidence as to whether the plans were their plans also. This must be recognized if we are to speak of the function and place of the layman in the parish, for this function and place must be given by the clergy: there must be the recognition of the joint partnership in being the people of God.

Assuming that this recognition is given, the next stage in the examination of the place of the laity in the parish is the consideration of the nature of the parish itself.

The Parish Itself. It has always been rightly said that if we are to know what our work is to be we must know not only the theology but also the situation, not only the principles of action but the place of action. So if we are to think of the place of the layman in the parish obviously a great deal will depend upon the nature of the parish. It may be a natural community such as a village or a small country town; it may be part of a larger community but still a community such as a cathedral city or a district of a great city, or it may be completely lacking in any sense of community at all, a large housing estate, a dormitory suburb to which people come to eat and sleep and to do little else. Then in addition to these facts there will have to be known certain facts about the parish. A sociological survey of the parish would be a good first beginning to know where the impact should take place: such facts as the principal occupation of the people living there, where the community life of the parish is to be found, are there any large scale factories or industries which absorb the majority of the people, what is the government of the parish in local politics, how is the parish represented in the local government, what are the needs of the parish in relation to housing, culture, companionships, what is the social stratification, are there any who live within but are outside the orbit of the majority of the people in their daily life and values.

It will obviously make a great deal of difference to the work and place of the laity whether or not the parish is a natural unit. If it is, then the work of the layman towards the community and towards the parish will be the same; but if the parish is simply, as it so often is in our large cities, simply a collection of streets around which the parochial boundaries are arbitrarily drawn, then obviously the work of the layman will lie far more in the community unit of the larger neighbourhood than in the narrow and arbitrary boundaries of the parish. This is one of the things we must learn to recognize, and one of the reasons why grouping of parishes is necessary so that the layman can exercise his function within the true community, which is probably a group of parishes of a deanery rather than the parish itself. This is sometimes a hard lesson for the clergy to learn, but it is quite absurd that the activities of Mr. Smith should be restricted to St. Clements just because he happens to live in the road which comes under St. Clements when his natural sphere of activity is the district of Afflueltham of which St. Clements is part.

The Church in the Parish. If a survey of the area is necessary in order that the layman may know where his impact is to be made, then equally it is necessary to assess the work which the Church is doing in the parish and whether that work has any real connection with the life of the place. The following seem to me to be the appropriate questions which each local church should ask itself and answer honestly:

a. How are we occupying the time of our people? Are we

expecting our lay people to spend all their evenings sitting on endless committees, the Church of England's self-appointed way of making sure that nothing is ever really done? or filling up every night of the week with clubs and organizations, and if so what functions are those organizations fulfilling in the making of new Christians, the training of present Christians, or towards the community which they serve? One man recently told me at a Lay Training Conference that in his parish at one time he sat on 17 committees, and when I look back at the life of All Saints, New Eltham, I am only too well aware of how much time of my own and of some of my best and keenest people I had to take up with such committee work.

b. Secondly we ask the question: is the local church an example of a living fellowship? Do people feel when they come into the life of the church that they are entering a community with a different mode of life and different scale of values from that of the world around them?—a community which is very conscious of being in the world yet not of the world, which is incarnate in the life as Christ was incarnate in life and yet has values which realize that here we have no abiding city. André Gide when he returned from Russia disillusioned said: "I went full of enthusiasm to admire a new world and they offered me to tempt me all the privileges and values which I most abhorred in the old world." I sometimes think that the same thing would happen to many who came full of enthusiasm into the life of our churches, expecting to find a new world full of new values, and then finding the snobberies, the class distinctions, the privileges jealously guarded, the struggles for power, which they most abhorred in the old world.

c. This leads me to the next question, which is a follow-up to that—is the local church in the true sense of that word offensive to the values of the community around it or has it sanctified the values of the world?

Peter Berger in his very worth-while book *The Noise of Solemn Assemblies*,[1] a sociological study of the Church in America,

[1] See above, p. 20.

says sadly that the Church in America has largely become a sanctification of the American way of life rather than of the Christian way of life. Kraemer in his book *A Theology of the Laity*[1] has said that the Western world is on the whole more dangerous than the Eastern Communist world to the life of the Church. This, he says, is because in the Communist world the Church is again in the state of being an offence, "the last enemy to be overcome on the road to a free religionless world, an enemy still to be reckoned with", whereas in the West the Church is not offensive but can quietly continue its life as it thinks fit, provided it does not meddle with the general affairs of the world in a way that is not considered useful. Anyone who has tried to be an offence to the world in Church Assembly will know what I mean by this. He says that this is dangerous for the Church because it is "constantly tempted to function as an ingredient and not as the salt of the world". In the local community we must be very careful if our Church too closely reflects in its people the sanctification of the British way of life, or the suburban way of life. To quote Kraemer again, "the modern world by its victorious secularism has domesticated the Church into a 'reservation' for the people with 'religious' needs and the Church has largely accepted this domestication."

Has the Church in your neighbourhood accepted this domestication? Have you as laity accepted the values or challenged the values of the neighbourhood in which you live?

d. The final question we must ask is this. Is the parish church outward-looking, fulfilling its ministry of service to the community? It is so easy for the local church and especially for the successful suburban church to be withdrawn from the world outside and immersed in a cosy and busy life of its own, catering largely for its own members. It is so easy to concentrate on being a good faithful member of one's church, dutifully paying one's membership fees by planned giving, spending most of one's time on church premises, that our ministry to the non-church member outside is largely forgotten and even sometimes excluded by the

[1] See above, p. 22.

emphasis on membership of the church organizations being limited to church-going people. A church can fall into the ultimate heresy which so many individuals fall into, of keeping itself to itself. Yet we must always remember that an essential part of the ministry is the ministry of diakonia, of being a deacon, not only in the technical sense of that word as the lowest order of full-time ministry, but in the sense of being a servant.

When Christ washed the disciples' feet He gave for all time an indication of the nature of Christian discipleship: that it is a discipleship of service. So the laity living in the world as an integral part of it is the primary body through which the reality of the phrase "the Church is diakonia", is service, has to be manifested in all spheres of secular life: the Church has to show in her own life and attitude towards others the evidences of the redemptive order which is in Christ an operative fact: Christ the Lord is also Christ the servant: the Church which is the lord of all life is also the servant of all life and the lordship is shown only through the service. The world wants to *see* redemption: it is not interested in being talked to about it. A church which is not outward-looking is a church which has ceased to be a church as the Body of Christ and has instead become a club for the benefit of its members.

The Function of the Layman in the Parish. In the light then of these considerations, both as regards the parish and the local church, let us now examine what the function of the layman is in the parish and what this will mean in terms of the life and ordering of our local church.

a. The layman must see himself as immersed in the situation of the world and of the parish. It is the layman above all other people who must come to grips with the situation in which he finds himself: it is he who living and working in the world daily experiences the gulf between what the Church stands for and what the world drives at. He is the one who is moulded and confused by the many different thoughts and trends of the world, and he can do one of two things. He can either develop a kind of dual standard, one for his life in the Church and another for his week-day life in the world, keeping the two strictly apart and adopting the world's standard of values for his daily life and the Church's standards for his church life; or he can try to be aware of and to express the relevance of the Christian faith to the very problems, difficulties and standards of the world in which he lives and works: to voice and incarnate Christ's relevance to the whole range of human life.

We need today a "holy worldliness", which seems to many a contradiction but is in fact not a contradiction at all. In fact the contrasting and contradicting of holiness and worldliness is the tragedy by which people often attempt to resolve the dilemma of Christian living. We live in two worlds—the world of our week-day life in which the standards of worldliness prevail, and the world of our church life in which for one day we try to live out the standards of holiness. We find a kind of peace, albeit an uneasy one, by accepting both worlds and keeping them strictly apart. We say "You can't be a Christian in business" and so we shut out Christianity on five days of the week, or we say "You can't mix politics and religion" and so treat political decisions as having no relevance in our personal living, or we say "human nature will out" and so divorce personal morality from religion. The Christian today is not called to a false separation between life and religion: he is neither called to be so identified with the world that he cannot speak to it, nor to be so remote from the world that it cannot speak to him. He is called to a "holy worldliness"—to the redemption of the world for Christ; as the Bishop of Woolwich says in his book *On Being the Church in the World*:[1] "The Church's task is to be wherever God is at work in the van of his process, baptizing and transforming it in Christ."

If our faith is not relevant to our daily life in the world and in the parish, then it is no use; and if we cannot be Christians in our work, in the neighbourhood, in our political decisions, then we had better stop being Christians. A piety reserved for Sundays is no message for this age.

[1] S.C.M. Press, 1960.

b. The layman has to be able to stand in the faith over against the values of the neighbourhood. We always have to remember that what we are speaks louder than what we say, and if we are going to make any kind of impact on our neighbourhood we have to show ourselves as people who have developed a Christian way of life and scale of values, who are not moulded by the world but moulders of the world in which we live.

If we consider the lives of Christians in their churches we so often find that they make good sons, fathers, husbands, employers and workmen—they have many individual virtues, but they have no way of life other than that which has been imposed upon them by their environment. It is their sociological conditions, their social class, their neighbourhood, their national characteristics rather than their Christian faith which determine their outlook and values: they are an overwhelming demonstration of the truth stated by Marx—that it is the economic conditions and background of a man's life which determine what he is and what he will think. This is an intolerable condition, and so long as it persists we shall not be able to make any impact on the world because it will be abundantly clear that it is the world which is making its impact upon us. And this problem of a people who have a definite Christian style of life, as Francis Ayres calls it in *The Ministry of the Laity*, is absolutely central; for it is at this point that the question of the integration of Christianity into the world, or at least of its creative power, will be most fiercely tested.

c. The function of the layman is also to be prophetic about the world in which he lives. By that I mean he must have a standard of judgment by which he looks at the world's problems and is enabled to bring to bear upon them the mind of Christ, so that when he speaks to his neighbours or in conversations at his work on the great issues of the world, political, economic or moral, he does not speak as a Conservative or a Socialist or as one thinking of his own interests, his class interests or even the nation's interests. Rather he will speak as one who is concerned primarily with the interests of a God who is at work in the world in which he is also at work, and who is in control of that world and seeking to redeem it.

As William Temple said, "God is not primarily interested in religion." He is interested in the world which He has created, into which He has come to be involved in His incarnation and which He has redeemed and now seeks to know and experience that redemption. If that is God's way it must be ours also. We must not be primarily interested in the political party we support, in the interests of our class, in the policies of our country, in the profits of our business organization, but in the work of God in all these spheres of life. This means that we must both learn from the world its complexity and the nature of its problems, which will mean a great deal of really objective study, and we must learn how to have dialogue or communion with that world with the mind of Christ. This does not mean guaranteeing that Christianity will solve all problems. It means simply and unpretentiously being the salt of the world, spreading light and illumination by helping ourselves and the world to put the right questions and seek the right answers.

d. Fourthly, it is the function of the layman in the parish to be aware himself as well as to make his clergy aware of the radical reorientation of outlook on their work together. Until now the average layman has looked upon his work in the Church as his spare-time activity and the work of the clergy as being the full-time work. This division no longer exists. Clergy and laity are no more and no less full-time than each other. If we think of the Church as simply the gathered congregation, then it is only at work on Sundays for a few hours and we might reasonably see ourselves then as partaking in a spare-time activity; but if we think of the Church as being the Body of Christ dispersed through the world from Monday to Saturday, then we are full-time workers in the Church wherever we are and whatever we are doing, and the layman is just as much working for the Church and being a minister where he is as is the clergyman where he is.

Further, this makes a great difference to the attitude of the laity and the clergy. The laity have only too often regarded themselves as being the passive recipients of what the clergy had to give them, and have waited for initiative from the clergy both in the ordering of the life of the local church and in the initiation of work in the neighbourhood; while the clergy themselves have only too often arrogated this position to themselves and have expected that the laity shall wait for the initiative from them, and have rather jealously guarded their work so that nothing happens unless they sanction it and in everything they must be the leaders. This position must be utterly broken down as soon as possible, so that there is no superiority whatsoever in being a clergyman over against a layman and no sense of the one being the leader and the other the passive receiver. Both are working together and learning from each other. The ministry of the laity is as constituent for the true being and character of the Church as the ministry of the clergy. Each is helping the other: the layman enables the clergyman to understand the complexities of the world in which he is situated, the world of which he knows far more than the clergy, the clergy are called to give to the laity the benefit of their theological understanding and so help them to account for and understand the faith which is in them.

The main part of the ministry of the clergy should be to enable the laity to fulfil their own peculiar inalienable ministry—the "laity are not the helpers of the clergy that the clergy may do their job but the clergy are helpers of the laity that the laity may *be* the Church". Moreover, the laity should never feel that it is an act of goodwill on their part to work for the Church and that they need to be appreciated and appealed to. To appeal to the laity with the request to be so kind and goodwilling as to help the Church is to deny what the laity are: the people of God sent into the world for witness and service. It is as much their duty as that of the clergy to give full-time work to the Church in the sense of witness to and service for the world. Many laymen find it a shock to realize that their loyalty to the Church is a loyalty prior to that which they owe their nation, business or even home; but it is so, and that is the meaning of so many of the sayings of Christ: "He that loveth father or mother more than me is not worthy of me"; "no man having set his hand to the plough and looking back is worthy of the kingdom"; or the parable of those who made excuses for their refusal to join the wedding feast.

The laity must then take their rightful place of leadership with and not below the clergy; claiming the right to initiate action, to decide for themselves what is the best form of service and not to be immersed in a host of organizations just because that is what the clergy conceive as working for the Church, seeking themselves to teach and be taught, working out with the clergy what is the best way to integrate faith to life and worship to life. It is a partnership of equals in which each has his own peculiar function but in which both are working as partners in a common concern—the redemption of the world, and working as common members of the whole people of God, the laos to which both clergy and laity belong.

What all this will mean in the practical life of the Layman in his Parish.

1. There will need to be a radical reorientation of the way in which the Church spends its time and a ruthless elimination of many activities, especially a radical re-examination of those which seek to concern themselves exclusively with membership of the Church. The Youth Club which will deal only with the nice, easy youth and refuses to accept the tough outsider; the Mothers' Union which closes its doors to women who cannot yet come within the orbit of the Church's communicant membership or are unable, through having failed in their marriages or in their morality, to enter its membership; the Church of England Men's Society which does not allow men who do not belong to the Church to have any share in its activities; all these must be very carefully examined as to whether they are a right use of church members' time or whether they are becoming nice little clubs for the mutual comfort and benefit of those who

B

already belong. We so easily tend to forget that the salt is only any good when it is no longer in the salt-cellar, the yeast when it is at work in the lump, the light when it is in a dark place. So we must remember that our life as church people is not to be lived within the walls of the church hall: excellent as our organizations may be, if they are not outward looking to the whole parish, to the ungodly as well as to the godly, then they are largely a waste of the precious time of which we have so little.

I would say that we ought to occupy a minimum of our laity in the running of such organizations, and that the vast majority within the life of the parish should be set free for experiments by which the life of the Christian and the thought of the Christian should be brought into touch with the life of the neighbourhood. Here is where our sociological surveys of the parish will come in, and I would suggest these patterns for work as lay people within the parish:

a. If the parish is also the natural local community then the majority should be at work in the local community life—taking their part in the borough councils, in the clubs which are for the whole community, in the organizations which minister to the whole community, in the local political parties rather than in any specifically church club. Thus the layman is being used for what he is, the salt out of the salt-cellar.

b. If the parish is not a natural community, then we may have to face the fact that we should release certain of our lay people altogether from the life of the local church, save for purposes of worship, in order to begin to make their impact on the wider world of the factories which serve the area or the wider districts in which the area organization will take place.

The Church so often refuses to recognize that a man may be doing his very best work for the Church when he is never seen within the walls of the church hall. Sometimes it even seems to resent that kind of person and to prefer the more clericalized layman who spends his entire spare time within the church organizations. These are of course necessary but they should not be the whole of the lay people within a church congregation. There will be those who have their main interests in the world outside the Church, but who by that very fact are learning what it is to be the Church in that world; people who are primarily engaged in their careers, in trade, in university teaching and life, in their schools, in different voluntary organizations outside the Church in local community centres, in local or national politics, or trade union organizations. If a man cannot come to church sometimes on Sundays because he has to attend a meeting of his union or his political party, then, provided he is conscious of his Christian vocation and calling to service within that body, he should be freed from church attendance without any sense of reluctance but rather with joyfulness and thankfulness that some members of the congregation are so immersed in holy world-liness.

Such people will learn what it means to be a Church permanently at work through the attitudes, insights, decisions and pressures of men engaged in political work, in board rooms, unions and workshops. An immense amount of influence can be brought to bear by men who have learnt what it means to be thinking about the problems of society in the light of their beliefs about man and the world. In fact, had there been more disciplined, concentrated and expert thinking by Christians on many social issues it is conceivable that a far greater unanimity upon many of them would have come about, and we should not be in this state of always having two opinions on almost everything political, economic, social and moral.

c. Whether the parish is a natural community or not, the actual work done by the laity in the parish will be directed always towards those outside the Church: therefore a much better direction for the work of the laity than keeping them within the four walls of church halls will be along the lines:

i. Of opening their homes for small group meetings of those within and without the local church. There is a great art in true hospitality; to make a fellow human being feel completely relaxed and at ease in one's presence and in one's own home springs from a radical humility which transcends self. To show genuine interest in one's neighbours and be truly considerate towards them, to use our homes as the church of the street or road and be equipped to lead others gently by conversation to the knowledge of Christ and the values of Christ, is the most effective work a layman can do.

ii. Of visiting within one's road, being the representative of the Church within the road, being aware of what is going on so that the needs of the lonely, the sick and the aged are met immediately with consideration and genuine concern: being much more concerned with what people are interested in and much less concerned with simply bringing them along to church but rather being the Church to them. As the Archbishop of Canterbury has said, we have to be less concerned with our people as "pew-fodder" and more concerned with them as persons, as people with their own interests, their own problems, their own joys.

iii. Of joining together with those of like occupations, whether it be through our knowledge of the occupations of the people within the parish or through cells or groups within the places of work; discussing together the common problems of the work upon which one is engaged with those inside and outside the Church who are engaged upon the same work; by building in the desert of modern life genuine cells of Christian conviction and purpose, interpenetrating the world and so communicating with it: that is the task of the Church.

2. The need of training and study will be much more part of the life of the layman in the parish and the need of training of ourselves to be the kind of people we are meant to be.

I shall not say a great deal about lay training, because that forms a separate paper, but I will say this at this point: that there should fall to the laity the work of teaching other laity in the parish, in study and discussion groups, what being the Body of Christ in the world really means, and this will involve serious discussion both of the Bible and of the concrete situations in life to which the message of the Bible has to be brought. So a great deal more time will have to be allowed for lay people to do this work and to be trained for it. The clergy will have to realize that the work of training the laity can be safely entrusted to other laity who have themselves received such training.

But the kind of training about which I will say something here and now is the training which is largely self-given: the training to be the kind of person who expresses the views of a Christian and not of the world in his private conversation and in his own scale of values. Here is where we have to be so careful. A writer in a magazine says that he was recently at a conference of young people from a very active church: they were discussing all kinds of deep spiritual problems at the conference but at the meal table their conversation consisted of jobs, better pay, love affairs, better prospects, getting on. When they were asked if they did not see some conflict between what they were discussing so abstractly and their actual daily concerns, they did not see the point. Devotional life was one thing, the rest of life was a matter of self-fulfilment.

This was also brought home by an experience at a recent lay training week-end. Discussing the Bible in the morning all the right things were said and the right values given, but when in the afternoon a real problem of expenses-fiddling and business interests was being discussed all sorts of social snobberies, worldly ideas, business is business etc., were revealed, because here they were discussing real life and here their real values came out. We have to be so sure that what we are is not being revealed much more when we are off guard in ordinary conversation and the ordinary crises of life than in the careful conversation within the walls of the Church. The real presence of Christian charity makes itself very apparent in ordinary conversation.

We need to train ourselves to be in these days people who:

i. Know how to listen to others.

ii. Know how to deal with people where they are and not where we want them to be.

iii. Have the right judgment on how to resist advertisement pressure and the other pressures of a conformist society.

iv. Know how to choose the right values in a world of abundance—not immediate satisfaction; know how to be free of the chains from which Christ would set us free—desire, lust for things—pride in possessions.

v. See other people as persons, neither making stereotypes, nor lumping people together into groups, Jews etc., but seeing each person as Christ sees them with separate identity and significance. This will all take a great deal of self-training and force us to get outside our normal prejudices and preconceptions and to try in our own lives to have the mind of Christ upon all things. A great deal of time will have to be spent in radical self-examination of our attitudes and values.

3. The laymen in the parish will have the work of seeing that their local church is indeed a community and serving the community needs.

The Church is intended to be a Christocentric community, but often it is nothing of the sort but rather a closed shop or a group of isolated individuals who neither know nor care for each other. Yet in a society of which the outstanding traits are loneliness and conformity there is a great need for real communities of mutual upbuilding, witness and service. As the Body of Christ, the Crucified, the Church cannot aim at conquering but must aim at interpenetrating the world and so communicating with it. The way for the institutional Church is to confront incessantly the official local congregations whether in urban, suburban or rural environments with the simple question: what does it involve to be a Christocratic brotherhood? Not a place where religion of a certain brand brings people together at stated times for stated activities, but a brotherhood where everybody finds his or her place and his or her task and where the creative fact is the living Christ, the Redeemer and Reconciler who wants to reach the world to minister to it through His redeemed.

Every layman should examine the life of his local church in this respect and his own attitude to people within it. It is true fellowship, true community? If someone needing love and care came into your church, would you be able to recognize the need and would you be able to give them the significance that they needed to have, the love for which they are desperately longing, the feeling that someone cares? It was said of the great priest, Fr. Wainwright, that while he lived no-one was friendless, no-one experienced the feeling that nobody cared whether he lived or died. Would that that could be said of each one of us! Only too often the complaint is heard that a person has been time and time again to a church and no-one, clergy or people, has spoken to them or welcomed them. I know that this is only our cursed English reticence, but let that reticence go, it isn't a good thing and is responsible for much loneliness.

Let there be also the realization that the Church is service and that this means service to the community without reservation and without conditions. Let there be within every church a roll of members willing to give service and the knowledge of the kind of service that is available, e.g. gardening, decorating, visiting lonely people, shopping for old people etc., and let there be those whose job it is to find out the needs and put the service to the need. Actions speak louder than words, and a church which is willing to give unselfish and disinterested service to fellow men, often without uttering one so-called religious word, is a church which is learning to be converted first to Christ and then to the world.

4. But the words "first to Christ" remind me of the last function of the layman which I would mention here—the function of the layman to work out with the clergy a pattern of worship and a pattern of lay-holiness which is applicable to the world in which we live.

Let there be no conservatism about worship. So often it is the laity themselves who refuse to make any changes in the ordering of things because that is what they have been used to. But the standard by which we judge our worship is not "what I have been used to" but what does modern man in the world of 1963 need if he is to see the relevance of worship and life and if the needs of his own soul are to be met? This means building up together, clergy and laity, a pattern of worship which aims at:—

a. Relating religion to life in every act of symbolism made and every word uttered.

b. Communicating the truths of the faith in a way that the modern world understands and in language which is comprehensible.

c. The ordering of worship in such a way that the wonder, the mystery and the homeliness of God are equally apparent.

d. The fullest possible participation of clergy and laity in the act of worship.

It means too that one of the most important things of today is to try to find what might be called a pattern of lay-holiness applicable to the modern age. An age in which we live against a background of noise needs to know how to use silence: an age in which there is a problem of time needs to rethink daily prayer in terms of a daily awareness of God rather than long and sustained prayers: an age which is used to simple and direct language needs a spiritual reading and prayers which are simple and direct: an age in which we are to work for the integration of religion and life needs the kind of prayer which relates religion and life. At a recent working party in the Bristol diocese of clergy and laity, the laity insisted that they did not want lectures to get them through "O" levels in religious knowledge but teaching soaked in practical prayer; they wanted to work out for themselves, but with the help of their clergy, what lay-holiness is, not monastic holiness or theological college holiness or clerical holiness but lay-holiness. Twentieth century Christians need twentieth century methods of prayer, a modern spirituality and holiness for life which is practical and realizable in the world of today. It would be a great thing if in every parish there were a group of laity working out together what they needed as a pattern of lay-holiness for life and for daily prayer and what this would also mean in the communal worship of the Church.

Conclusion. To summarize then: if we would know the place of the laity in the parish we must first seek to know by survey the nature of the parish itself, to question what the Church is doing and being in the life of the parish; then in the light of these findings seek to see yourself as involved in a decisive dialogue with the world in which you are supremely the Church yet called to stand over against the values of the world, and to speak to the world, and called to do this together with the clergy and not under the direction of the clergy, taking the initiative yourselves in this your own special task. This will mean in practice a radical reorientation of the way in which the Church spends its time, the examination and pursuit of ways by which you as the Church may permeate the life of the community, training yourself to be involved in the world as a member of Christ and to be the kind of person in values that a member of Christ is meant to be, seeing that your Church is a community and looks out to the needs of the community, and finding the pattern of worship and holiness which befits you and your contemporaries in the modern world.

This is a tall order, for it means that you are called to be reconciler in the conflicts that separate men and men, questioning the world incessantly and inducing it to put the right questions in regard to its problems: letting yourself, the world and the Church stand under the divine judgment and throughout all this sounding in your life and service the note of the certainty of God's triumphant love. But this is what it means to be the people of God. This is what it means to get on with the job of being Christians living in the world, not people living in the world who are also in their spare time Christians, but Christians informing their daily activities with the mind of Christ. A man once said to me: "I don't question that the Church is *speaking* the truth; what makes me angry is that the Church is not *living* it." It is when the world sees you living it that you will begin to make an impact on the world.

3

THE PLACE OF THE LAITY IN THE PARISH (ii)

by

LESLIE PAUL

IN GENERAL THE mark of the Anglican laity for more than two centuries past, let us say since the seventeenth century, perhaps excepting the Wesleyan movement, has been its passivity.

When the parish vestry had real responsibilities in local government, this passivity was in some sense mitigated. Lay activity was channelled into local politics and social service, but with the abolition of the local government function of the vestry, even this outlet for lay activity and lay initiatives disappeared. In my view this passivity has been reinforced by the nature of the Church as it must have appeared to generations of laity since the languishing of the great debates of the seventeenth century. It came to appear and must appear still as a "given" thing. As far as the laity could see, the Church was not simply established but *provided*.

The fact that it was the instrument through which a parishioner made his worship did not alter its providential nature. Its liturgy was given by the law, its head was the crown, its officers were appointed and promoted and maintained by processes so tortuous and secretive that no layman (and very few clergy either) could really hope to understand them, let alone control them. And moreover, for this history-given and state-given corporation the rank-and-file of the laity was not expected to pay. True, it was exhorted to subscribe to the collections, and to put its hand in its pocket for missions and so forth, but paying for *the church and the minister* in the sense of providing them did not occur, and still in general does not occur today. Then again, this lay passivity was further encouraged by the fact that the Church and the laity were organically separate. The phrase "entering the Church", meaning ordination, exactly summed up the situation between the Church as a corporation and the laity as a non-entity. The Church, and its officers, were a corporation apart from the laity. Basically they still remain so.

Of course, the laity were the necessary "customers", but the customers are not the same thing as the business, as a glance at Woolworth's or Sainsbury's reminds us. There have always been exceptions to the remoteness and passivity of the laity in, for example, churchwardens and other prominent laymen who tend to constitute a kind of privileged laity. Kraemer, I think, calls them a *clericalized* laity, and discusses whether to include them in the category of ministry. Actually they form an N.C.O. class really, and therefore are almost as remote from the laity as the clergy itself, just as the N.C.O. is as remote from the privates that he has to drill as he is from the officers he must obey. The fact that other lay people have to look after the church flowers, or run bazaars, or the Sunday School, does not really make them any more members of the corporation than the schoolboy who is made secretary of a school club is by that fact made a member of the school staff. He still remains a pupil. The revealing fact is that the laity have seldom been used in the past, and are seldom used by the Church today, in church affairs at the level of their ability in secular affairs.

I may illustrate this by a story. When I came out of the forces and settled down in Battersea I went to the church at the corner. I was the only lay *man* in the congregation. There were two laymen in the choir: they were father and son, and they constituted the whole of the choir. They sat up there in the chancel in their cassocks and surplices; I sat down in the pews with the bulk of the congregation, but there wasn't a bulk—just a scattering of old ladies. Now, Sunday after Sunday for several weeks after I arrived, the parson preached about the absence of lay help in the parish, particularly from lay *men*, and, poor chap, he'd look around for the laymen to accuse of this, and he could find only me. So his sermon every Sunday was preached against me, until I went and asked him how I might help, and was told that I might become a server. Well, I did, and continued to be one for very many years: but it was hardly a case of stretching me to the level of the performance the secular world asked of me.

The illustration of the schoolboy who is secretary of the school club and does not by that fact become a member of the school staff is a happy one, because it helps to reveal the relationship between the clergy and the laity which resembles the relation between the teacher and the taught. The laity is still *in statu pupillari*, because it is faced with a priesthood which is a professional body, cut off from the rest of the laos by several things. Unless we face the fact that the priesthood is a professional body, we don't really come to grips with the problem of the relationship between the laity and the priesthood as it is and as it ought to be.

Now what are the things that, so to speak, cut the laity off from the ordained ministry? Well, of course, first there is the professional training of the clergy. Without doubt the young man coming out of theological college feels himself a member of a group or a class apart, and this is reinforced by all that follows: the ordination ritual, post-ordination training, clerical dress, the pattern of the clerical life. Professional training leads naturally to a considerable professional selfconsciousness. If you listen to the debates in the House of Clergy, and in the Church Assembly (where they are to some extent chastened by the presence of the laity), you will see that the clergy think as a professional group. The debate recently on the question of a central registry really showed all the anxieties and the self-consciousness of a professional group which was not going to have any kind of central examination of its local situation and of its professional record.

In the face of this professionalism, the layman is really very much in the situation of the chap who tries to run his own legal affairs. If you try and say as a layman in law what you think your solicitor or your barrister ought to do, you are immediately up against a great professional barrier. The lawyers have the know-how and you don't. The layman has this same feeling about the priesthood in general, that the priesthood has been given the know-how and is in possession of it, and the laity does not have this know-how and therefore is embarrassed and diffident: it does not have the language: it cannot bring up against the professionalism of the clergy its own professionalism, only its amateurism.

That is not the total situation, by any means. The clergy is not only a professional group: it is a priestly group: and we ought not to underestimate the sense in which as a priestly group it is set apart. Perhaps it ought not to be set apart, but it is set apart. It is set apart just as the church building is. The one is set apart by consecration, and the other by ordination. Priesthood is a seal for life, and part of the obligation of priesthood is not to indulge in certain occupations which might be held to be degrading for a priest but not for a layman. If the priesthood is set apart in a truly holy sense, then it is set apart by God, and in the eyes of layman and priest some divinity brushes off onto the priesthood.

I know that many may object to so absolute a sanctification which is not also a sanctification of the laity; but you have to reckon here not simply with the attitude of the priest himself, but also with an attitude of long standing on the part of the laity towards the priesthood. The recent C.A.C.T.M. Report, *Gender and Ministry*, says : "Many devout church people are truly in the dark, baffled by the fact that the Church gives the recognition of Holy Orders to only one ministry, out of the many to which Christians as the Body of Christ are called. Many would receive fresh encouragement to be better people in their own spheres if the too-prevalent attitude towards the clergy as the recipients of some semi-magical status could be clearly and forcibly disclaimed, discouraged and discarded. "A remarkable statement—but notice that the Report says *if* this sense of semi-magical status could be discarded. It has not been discarded yet. It still is true that in the minds of the mass of the laity, or at least of those who are conscious of it at all, the parson is a chap set aside in a sacred way difficult in practice to distinguish from a magical way, as the church building is set aside in a sacred way. I can illustrate this by a story about the delightful church to which I still belong. I remember the most furious arguments one day in the vestry between the servers as to whether the servers could touch the Communion vessels, and the absolute paralysis of a server when, after consecration, some Breads were dropped on the altar carpet. Should he pick them up, or should he leave them where they were?—because these were part of the sacred elements which had been consecrated by the priesthood, and therefore all this belonged to the particular dimension of the sacred, in which only the priest could function.

These may seem to be somewhat eccentric examples, but they are not. I am sure that this attitude is far more widespread than we imagine it to be, and I am sure that the priesthood has to a very great extent itself lived upon this particular ethos of the Church.

Then, among other things which set the priesthood apart from the laity, we have to reckon with class separation and intellectual separation. Perhaps these are factors which are on the way out now, but it is not necessarily so in working class areas or housing estates where, as somebody has already said, the priest appears as one coming from the outside, not produced within the group, within the laity, within the laos, but coming from another social world, and as it were inducted into his powers and his separateness by a bishop, and with all the authority of this great and distant corporation (as the laity sees it) behind him. Class separation, social separation, intellectual separation, even if diminishing, are still real barriers.

Then there is something which sets the parson still further apart, and that is his independence, established by the freehold, which enables him to defy his flock or to ignore it. I am not going to say that the average parish priest does defy his flock or ignore it, but we all know cases where he virtually retires and shutters himself up, provides the statutory services, and goes his own way. If parishioners complain they learn, "Well, he can't be moved: you see, it's the parson's freehold." And this is the kind of thing that gets around and people come to accept that the mysterious power a parson has to be his own fortress against the world is one more thing which separates him from the world everyone else lives in. And of course it has been noticed that in this situation he enjoys a security of tenure that nobody else enjoys in any other kind of job except, conceivably, the civil servant.

Let me say this about the Church of England in general: the parson shares the mystery which belongs to the whole corporation. It is really frightfully difficult to understand how the Church of England works, or even whether there is one Church of England and not six or seven different centres of power even in the central church, and perhaps forty-three if you count each diocese as a separate centre of power. For the ordinary layman and for masses of parsons too, this really is a stumbling block. The Church cannot be grasped intellectually, it cannot be grasped organizationally, it cannot be understood in the way it works perhaps even by those very near to the centre of it. I speak feelingly here, having to try to discover just this fact in order that I may make my Survey.

Now of course some of the things which cut the parson off from his laity have been changed, or are in the process of being changed by organizational efforts of one kind or another, ever since the Life and Liberty movement. We are all familiar with the new role of the parochial church councils, of Church Assembly, the House of Laity and perhaps the new movement to introduce houses of laity into the Convocations. But admirable as these efforts are in creating grass roots democracy in the Church, if they are not really as yet successful it is again because of the extraordinary complexity of the Church. It is really very difficult for a P.C.C. (parochial church council) to know how, in fact, to bring within its grasp problems which face the whole Church, or how to make its views and its will felt. And so it is apt to limit its concern to things just at the parish pump level. In any case, many P.C.C.s have met the parson who says, "Oh, well, this is my concern and it has nothing to do with the P.C.C., and I don't like to discuss it."

The stewardship campaign has proved a remarkable effort to break down the isolation and the passivity of the laity, and where it has been tried out it has, as far as one can see, been phenomenally successful. But it is very interesting that in the stewardship campaign quite often what have been harnessed to the service of the Church are the professional skills which the laity exercise in their secular callings, and it is therefore a sign to us that there may be other professional skills, not simply money-making skills, that we can hope to harness to the Church's service.

Well, there are theological efforts to create new attitudes. Far be it from me to trespass upon the fine address of the Bishop of Woolwich, but in this post-war concern with the role of the laity certain phrases keep cropping up, such as "the priesthood of all believers" or doctrines of the mystical body, and these seek to put the situation theoretically right. But phrases, even good theological phrases, do not really necessarily change anything, and one of my fears is that they can often only be just phrase-making, covering the realities with a smoke-screen. And in that connection I think often of the procession up my church aisle on a Sunday morning of two members of the youth club, or two elderly parishioners, bearing the Elements: and this strikes me as an unreality. True, it gives the laity a ceremonial role, but the truth is we have not presented these Elements. Somebody, the priest or the churchwarden, has been off and bought them, and has prepared our "gift" for us. We have put ourselves to no trouble. Now if it really were the case that we *could* present the Elements, I think I should be very glad to get a little group together and buy a bottle of Nuits St. Georges, and come up with some bread freshly baked. Then really we should have *presented* something, instead of the modern elaborate way of pretending to present something. So I think we ought to be aware of the possibility that even in new lay roles like that, which have an admirable intention, we may be producing a new sort of hypocrisy about what we are doing.

Well, let me now come to something practical. I do believe that there is a genuine movement in the Church under way, and that the next great transformation could be over the role of the laity, though I don't say necessarily that it will be. I think it ought to be. But if this is to come about, if there is to be a revolution over the role of the laity, then a new professionalism of the laity has to be born. I do not wish to write off the professionalism of the clergy, despite what I may have said about it. It needs to be more thorough and effective, but one certainly needs to step up, in contrast, the professionalism of the laity, in independence of the clergy. Almost every lay movement in the Church seems to be clerically sponsored and led—even this one! And I want to see, as the first condition of the success of this lay revolution, a lay movement which sees itself as the laity, coming together as laity, first to understand what the laity is for, and what it has to do, and has to learn, and which only then is prepared to go to the clergy and say, "Where do we go from here?" or "Let's discuss this", instead of endless well-meaning clerical patronage under which the lay people are told who they are, and what they ought to be, and what they should do, but never, as it were, produce the initiatives themselves. And I want this right down through the machinery of the Church to the parishes, lay councils, lay chapters, and when necessary separate educative or educational sessions of the laity of the P.C.C.

I suppose what I want is a "people into the parish" movement with the life of Christian Action and the brains of Christian Frontier—you notice the subtle distinction—and the spur to reform of the Keble Conference or maybe the William Temple Association—all members of these organizations please note. But what I also want now and immediately is something perhaps even more practical: a nationally organized and locally functioning movement (and these two things are important) to be called

Lay Voluntary Service, which can perform for and within the Church the kind of things the Women's Voluntary Service has done so admirably over the years—cars, chauffeurs, advice, secretarial help, cleaning and decorating, gardening groups that come at call, and that kind of thing. And this really springs from the need I see to bring secular skills and energies to the rescue of a clergy which is often physically worn out, burdened with enormous physical tasks. So many parsons are their own vergers, their own gardeners, sometimes possibly their own gravediggers.

If you simply have a movement of the laity which is going to try to think up what the laity's tasks are, and nothing more, you might have something like the relationship between the Ford workers and the management of Ford's as the ultimate outcome. But if you also carry it along with a "self help for the Church" movement, then it is possible to create a new brotherhood of the laity and of the clergy together through service and co-operation and the integration of common tasks. Also, I think, such a movement might help to smooth away the resentments which are bound to be stirred up in the clergy as a professional group, not just as individuals, at first at any rate, by a laity which shows the new measure of independence for which I ask.

4

THE LAYMAN'S PLACE IN CHURCH GOVERNMENT

by

PETER WHITELEY

THE IDEA THAT the laity have a place in church government is not, of course, new. In the past, parliament was intended to be representative of the laity in the Church. But for historical reasons reality ceased to correspond to this theory, and towards the end of the last century there grew up a movement for separate representation of the laity, that is, separate not so much from the clergy as from parliament. This movement culminated in the Enabling Act of 1919, which set up the Church Assembly.

I suppose partly as a result of the prayer book controversies of 1927/28 there has since been a growing desire for further changes, and part of this whole movement for further changes has been an increased understanding of the part that laity can and should play in the whole process of church government. This is sometimes argued on grounds of democracy, but I think we are on very dangerous ground here, because the Church is not a democracy. The Church is, among other things, a closely related body of separate but distinct elements, and any system of church government must, in my view, recognize the existence of these separate elements, but also provide for their efficient functioning together. The place of the laity in church government does not depend on any theory of democracy, but on the fact that they are one of these essential elements. The Church consists, among other things, of bishops, clergy, and laity: and I would suggest that any system of government that does not provide for proper representation of the laity is in fact defective. If it is true, as it obviously is, that the laity can err without the counsel of bishops and clergy, I think that it is also true that the bishops and clergy can err without the informed consent and understanding of the laity. I am not for one moment suggesting that when all three are together we shall produce an infallible system of government, but there seems at least less chance that we shall produce decisions that are wrong.

Now when considering the whole process of church government one is obviously struck by its growing complexity and the increasing amount of time that it requires. This is referred to elsewhere in this book, and it is common knowledge that at the national level the Church Assembly now sits for approximately three weeks in the year. This is not the moment to discuss details of organization, though I do think some streamlining is possible, particularly at the national level, in the way that the whole system works. But we have got to face the fact that any dramatic changes are unlikely. It might be possible to reduce the time required from three weeks to two, but I think it is unlikely that we shall achieve anything very drastic in this connection. Moreover, at the diocesan level, as I shall suggest a little later on, I think that probably we have got to devote more time to church government rather than less.

This undoubtedly presents us with a problem which I think we must be prepared to face at the outset. All of us accept that the layman's chief vocation is in the world: in the factory, in the office, on the farm, in the home, in the school, or wherever it may be. Recently in my own diocese a suggestion was made that we might hold a diocesan conference on Sunday, and it was rather depressing that one or two priests, though by no means all, argued against this on the grounds that their particular vocation had its crown, its culmination, on Sundays. But they failed to appreciate that a layman's vocation probably has its crown or culmination on weekdays, and that participation in any form of church government does in fact provide, if not a crisis of conscience, at least a problem of conscience to all of those who are considering it. Nevertheless, I would like to suggest that there are possibly three reasons why lay people should seriously consider taking part in church government and church administration.

First, I think most of us accept that there is considerable value in what might be called additional good works: by this I mean additional to our everyday life. Probably the majority of Christians do accept this, and play a part either in some recognized church work or in local government, or in one of the voluntary organizations. I think this may help to provide a sense of proportion and balance in one's everyday work, and I don't think that it needs to be argued very strongly. I am, however, equally convinced that it is not a conclusive argument.

The second reason why the laity should consider entering all forms of church government is quite simply because church government and administration are important, particularly so at this moment. The structure and the organization of the Church is changing; the central administration of the Church is growing. I see nothing wrong in this. It tends to grow in the hopes that it will provide greater efficiency. But it is vital that it should be efficient, and that we should all be concerned to make it so.

Now my third reason for urging the participation of the laity in church government is far and away the most important. Other essays in this book have mentioned the quality of the membership of the Church Assembly, and we probably all have our own views on the quality of the membership of our diocesan conferences. Most laity in church government tend to be those who have retired or have private means. This is obviously not completely true; there are a number of young people in the Church Assembly, and probably a number of young people in every diocesan conference. Nevertheless it is generally true that those who take part in church government are those who have retired, or have private means, and therefore do not have to have a full time job. But if the layman's primary vocation is in the factory or in the office or in the school, then surely it is precisely these laity who are most required in the whole system of church government. It is their insight, their knowledge, their skills and perhaps even more important, their impatience, their desire to get something done, that could illuminate and vitalize the whole process of church government.

I think this is by far and away the most important point I am trying to make. The laity have an essential part to play in church government because they are an essential part of the Church. But the laity most required are those who often have least time to give, and I would therefore like to suggest that all who find themselves in this position should at least consider whether it is possible to reorganize certain aspects of their lives to enable them to play their part in this highly important work.

Having now considered some of the essential elements of church government, and the layman's part in it, I would like to go into it in a little more detail, and it is probably convenient to do it at the three levels of parochial, diocesan and national.

Elsewhere in this book there is a considerable amount of discussion on church government at the parochial level and the layman's part in it. I think it is generally agreed that whatever the formal structures of church government at that level, it depends tremendously on the personal relationship between the parson and his parishioners, and particularly his more committed church members. The parochial church council is of course intended to help in the running of the whole parish, but it is probably at this level that the tension can be most acute between the particular pastoral responsibility of the priest and the overall evangelistic responsibility of the whole Church in that particular locality. In theory, of course, these two do not conflict. But in practice, no matter how wrong a priest's views may be on how to deal with some pastoral problem, they will tend to prevail. Or, to put it the other way, if the laymen of the parish particularly want to do something they are very unlikely to succeed if they do not receive the support of the incumbent. I speak with a little hesitancy here, because my own experience is almost entirely in small country parishes, and I imagine that in big town parishes things may be very different. In a small country parish the whole idea of synodical government has a dream-like quality. At home I doubt whether we have ever had a proper election to the P.C.C., because the constitution of our parochial council provides for almost as many members as there happen to be regular church-goers. There was a suggestion a little time ago that we should in fact have an election because there appeared to be one man over. We finally decided that it would so embarrass the one person who was not elected that it was all cosily arranged that someone should stand down in rotation.

Another point made elsewhere in this book, which I would nevertheless like to repeat, is that one of the factors that militates against the development, not only of parochial church government, but of the whole acceptance of joint responsibility by parson and laity, is the parson's freehold. It is not a question that I am going to discuss in any detail because it is, perhaps, contingent rather than central to what we are now considering. But I am quite convinced that it does put the parson in a peculiar category in the eyes of many laymen. Equally important, I think, it allows some of us laymen to sidle out of our responsibilities because we can be given the impression that the laity are not trusted. I feel that the laity may not accept their full responsibilities in the parish until the present system is at least modified.

The most important area, however, for the development of church government is the diocese. The diocese is the basic unit of our church—the basic unit of any episcopal church. Moreover, it is large enough to develop and support all sorts of experiments and forms of pastoral and evangelistic work. Most parishes are not in this position because they can only draw on inadequate funds, but a diocese should be, and frequently is, rich enough to experiment in all sorts of ways. That is one side of the picture.

In practice, however, it is at diocesan level that synodical government is least effective. In many dioceses it is practically non-existent. This is particularly tragic because it is the level at which many laity could play the greatest part and have the greatest impact. There is a far greater chance in the dioceses than at national level. There laymen have some really intimate knowledge of the problems under discussion. There is also the very important practical point—it is far easier for most people to get to diocesan meetings, which can possibly be held in the evenings, than to come to Church Assembly for three weeks in the year. In addition, I personally believe that participation in diocesan government can be immensely rewarding. It is often possible to achieve a greater sense than at national level of personal responsibility for seeing particular results achieved. If, at a diocesan conference, a layman supports a proposal requiring money, there is not the slightest doubt that he bears considerable personal responsibility to ensure that his parish pays up its own contribution. At national level, however, the responsibility to see that one's own diocese makes its full contribution to central funds is shared, perhaps, with a dozen diocesan representatives to Church Assembly. Therefore I do suggest that at diocesan level one can achieve a great sense of personal responsibility.

Recently, at my own diocesan conference, we passed a budget which was not only considerably in excess of last year's but several thousand pounds in excess of what has actually been achieved last year. There was some dispute as to whether this was an act of sublime faith or grossest irresponsibility. But I don't think there is any doubt that every member of that diocesan conference bears a considerable amount of personal responsibility to see that his own parish pays its full share to that budget.

Whatever the result in that instance, however, it is generally agreed that diocesan conferences are ineffectual. There are probably three reasons for this. The first is the obvious one—they are too large and unwieldy, and usually meet for two afternoons or at the most two days in the year.

Secondly there is this continual problem of the quality of the lay membership. There is this crying need for men and women of imagination to come forward and play their part in diocesan conferences. Their present lack, however, may partly result from the third reason why diocesan conferences tend to be ineffectual, and that is their lack of real power, particularly vis-à-vis the diocesan bishop. This may well inhibit busy people from joining diocesan conferences.

It was interesting to discover in the Church of England Year Book that the description of the powers and functions of a parochial church council take two-thirds of a page, while those of a diocesan conference can be described in a quarter of a page. Nevertheless, the diocese offers considerable scope for the development of proper synodical government, partly for the practical reasons that I have already given—that it is easier to organize meetings and get people to attend them. I think there are, however, two other reasons. First, although the diocese is *the* basic unit of the Church, it has tended not to be a unit for doctrinal decisions. This, at present, is the prerogative of the whole Church, and is discussed and decided at provincial and national level. Now I am aware that if the proposals of the report of the Joint Committee of the Convocations on Synodical Government are put into effect this situation may change. On page 9 of this report it is suggested that on major doctrinal matters reference should be made to the dioceses, and that half the dioceses have got to accept any particular change. I myself am not entirely happy about this suggestion. There is obviously considerable disagreement on the final place of the laity in doctrinal decisions, and it would be a pity if disputes on this matter held up the whole development of synodical government at diocesan level. But anyway, at present, this is not something that takes place. Diocesan government on the whole can avoid doctrinal decisions, and this is one of the reasons why I feel that it is ripe for a considerable degree of development.

The second reason, which is somewhat paradoxical, is that the episcopate is nearly monarchical. There are only two major checks on the power of the diocesan bishop. One is the parson's freehold, and when that is modified I do not wish to see it placing more power in the hands of the diocesan bishop; the other is the necessity for the bishop to come to a diocesan conference to raise money for any scheme that he may wish to undertake. But even here he has the initiative in most major schemes, and it is by no means easy at the diocesan conference to get up and oppose something that a bishop is suggesting. The bishop is able to say: "I have consulted with my archdeacons: I have got planning permission." If it is a matter of dealing with a new school and church he may have had discussions with the Ministry of Education, or with this or that authority, and if one has not got this background information it is not always very easy to oppose him. Moreover, there are many members of the diocesan conference who will tend to regard it as impertinent to oppose anything that a bishop suggests.

But the very fact that the bishop has got this considerable power means that if he wished he could develop church government at the diocesan level without reference to anyone— certainly, as far as I am aware, without reference to parliament. He could, in fact, voluntarily agree to share his powers with some from of diocesan council consisting of both clergy and laity. I certainly think the members of the bishop's "court" —the arch- deacons and other officials—will have to sit on it, which may well mean that there is a preponderance of clerical representation. But there should also be a large element of elected laity and elected clergy, elected by the diocesan conference and responsible to the diocesan conference. Such a council could meet regularly once a month, or even more often, and could discuss and advise on almost all major matters of diocesan policy. I do not think it is asking too much for the laity to play their part in such a council, for it would take no more time than many people are already prepared to give to local government and to various other forms of voluntary work.

I would like now to pass on to the national level (one might say the provincial level, but in practice the problems of church government at provincial level are not so very different from those at national level, and in addition, at the moment there is no lay representation at provincial level). Now if diocesan church government is important because the diocese is the basic unit of the Church, obviously church government at national level is equally important. A great deal of what is done at diocesan level is clearly affected by decisions taken at the centre, and the whole shape of the Church can be influenced by national decisions. It is true that there are sometimes criticisms of the growing centralization of church government and organization, but I think it is recognized, as I suggested earlier, that the aim of this is increased efficiency. It is inevitably taking place in most secular organizations, and I see no particular reason why the Church should believe that it can opt out of this process. In addition, it is probably important for the Church to have central organizations to be able to deal with the central secular organizations—the Church Information Office to deal with the national press; the Board of Education to deal with the Ministry of Education. But it is essential that the growing centralization of the Church in terms of government and administration should be both efficient and theologically sound.

I would suggest there are certain arrangements at present that are not theologically sound, and very definitely open to criticism. Probably the most glaring of these concerns the fact that our relations with other churches is decided unilaterally by the clergy, although this is something that affects the whole Church intimately. At present whether or not we join in communion or inter-communion with the Church of North India or South India, or wherever it may be, is a decision taken by convocations, without any reference to the laity.

Then there is the whole process of the revision of Canon Law. Here the laity have achieved the right to be consulted, though it is somewhat in the nature of a concession, and is by no means completely established. Not only is there a risk that this present position may be untheological, it is also highly inefficient. The clergy and the laity discuss matters of Canon Law independently of one another, with the result, of course, that the House of Laity gets in a shambles. Certainly laymen are not theological experts, but this is an added reason why discussions on things like Canon Law should take place with the clergy and laity seated together, simply so that the laity have a chance to listen to the arguments and to understand what the clergy are putting across.

Now, although there is much in the present system of central church government, and indeed in government at diocesan level, that is wasteful and deficient in the responsibilities which by and large it gives to the laity, I am quite certain this does not justify the attitude of indifference of the whole Church to church government, and in particular to the Church Assembly. Certainly the Church Assembly can be criticized. It is criticized elsewhere, and nobody knows better than those of us who are members of it how regularly and how rightly it requires criticism—for the quality of its membership, its lack of courage, its false sense of priorities, and perhaps most important, its fear of the establishment, both ecclesiastical and secular. But for this the whole Church must bear a very considerable measure of responsibility. You may remember that in the report of the Joint Committee on Synodical Government something was repeated from the Church and State Commission of 1935, which said that no electoral system could make the House of Laity or any other body fully representative of those who refrain from taking any active part or interest in its working. The most that an electoral system can do is to afford to all qualified persons who desire it a reasonable opportunity of being represented, and I think this is very, very true today.

One of the problems of Church Assembly is quite simply the lack of interest people are prepared to take in it. I think that the quality of its membership may in fact change as the power of the Assembly grows, particularly in relation to parliament. But I think we should also acknowledge that the Church Assembly already has quite considerable power to influence the shape of the Church. I will just give one example. As you probably know, Mr. Leslie Paul is carrying out investigations on the deployment and the payment of the clergy in response to a motion moved by a member of the House of Laity, Col. Madge. Whether or not we act on the results of this survey will depend a great deal on the Church Assembly and the quality of its membership, and on this will depend, in my view, much of the pastoral and evangelistic work of the Church, possibly over the whole of the next century. Is this the sort of decision that is going to be influenced by a courageous, forward-looking laity? (And I think I should also say at this point that in many of the things that come before us, the House of Clergy appear very much less conservative than the House of Laity.)

I began by suggesting that it is because of the nature of the Church that church government without the full participation of the laity is, in a sense, defective. I have also tried to argue that the laity most required are those who are still fully engaged in life. But is this simply a theoretical conception, or can we try and give it some practical application?

I suppose that all through the ages people have believed that they stood at the cross-roads of history. Nevertheless, I am sure that the next few years are going to be critical for the Church. I think they will show whether the Church is prepared to transform itself for mission in the modern world, or whether it is going to turn in on itself, afraid to change. If we want our church to live up to its responsibilities I am certain that we must use all means available to make it do so—we must write, we must argue, we must talk, we must work. I would also suggest that we have got to be prepared to work through and with the existing organs of church government at parochial, diocesan and national level. Moreover we must be ready to throw our inhibitions to the winds. At the moment there is a feeling that church politics, to be moral, must be dull and cosy and respectable. There is a feeling that people who go in for church politics or church government must be decently self-effacing. I believe this is absolute rubbish. If we believe that church reform is important, we must be prepared to fight for it. I believe we must try and see that at the next election of the House of Laity in three years' time there is somebody elected from every diocese who is prepared to speak for it, work for it and vote for it in the Church Assembly.

I know that the word "party" has somewhat dirty connotations in the Church of England. Nevertheless, I think we should recognize one thing at least about the existing parties, and that is that they have the honesty to organize for what they believe, and surely we must be prepared to do the same? Furthermore, the whole movement for radical reform in the Church cuts across the old party values—this is one of the exciting things about it—and I believe that a new party is now needed to work through the existing organizations until better ones are provided, to work for the reform of the Church of England.

5

THE LAYMAN AND CHURCH GOVERNMENT

by

MICHAEL BRUCE

I SHOULD HATE anyone to be misled into thinking that I have not got very strong and very deeply based opinions about this subject: "The layman's place in church government". I served on the Committee concerned with synodical government. I am a highly prejudiced and opinionated person. There was a minority report—I signed it. There was appended to the minority report a further note by a minority of one—I was that minority.

I want to take a long look at the word "government" before I get on to anything else, because I believe there are very important differences between, shall we say, the government of the Church, the government of the State, the government of a trade union, or a school, or a football club, or a family.

What does the word "government" really mean? Well, let us start at the beginning. Man was created in the image of God, and this does not just mean that *men* were created in His image. Man in that text means mankind as a whole; and that of course includes women. And it doesn't just mean that men and women as individuals were created in the image of God; it means that mankind, as mankind, was so created. So that the unity of Man ought to reflect the unity of God in love.

That kind of unity of mankind, reflecting the perfect unity of the Holy Trinity, is obviously something that just doesn't happen.

Man is divided by self-interest instead of united by love: divided by sin and by the abuse of freedom. So we get the law. If it weren't for that division the world would be governed by men looking up to and reflecting, imitating, the nature of God, which is love. But since man is fallen, we have both the Gospel and the Law. The Law and the Gospel govern our mutual relationships one with another. I think we see something of a parallel with all this if we take one of the kinds of government that I mentioned at the beginning—the human family. It is sometimes said, in relation to the government of the family, that if you give your children a good example you never need to punish them. It's awful nonsense. It is usually an excuse by parents for sliding out of one of the most difficult parts of their responsibility as parents. But after all, it can be put the other way. You get nonsense on the other side. I remember in my teens visiting a family: I met the father, and I suppose, as I was the Rector's son, he thought it necessary to apologize to me for the fact that he hadn't been to church recently. But then he went on to excuse himself by saying that the previous Sunday he had found that his eldest daughter had gone for a walk when she ought to have been at Sunday School, and she had got the strap. When I duly reported this to my father he said: "Mmm, it is some time since he was in church; I've been here for twenty years, and I haven't seen him yet." You can, you see, substitute punishment for example, and that is nonsense too. In fact, in the human family you need both.

But I believe, even in the natural family, that example is the dominant factor, and this certainly is true of the Christian family. In the government of the Christian family, example is more important than punishment.

Now in church government we are concerned primarily with what corresponds to the example side of things in the human family, with the response that we ought to make to the love of God. Our primary concern is to reflect the nature of God. Christ became man in order that he might redeem men from their fallen state, from their selfishness and self-isolating divisions from God and from each other; so that gathered together in one in

Him, man may offer to God that likeness to Himself in love for which he was created. Church government is primarily concerned with this; with worship, with the drawing of the whole life of the whole world into this reflection of the nature of God. It is secondly and only secondly concerned with the quarrels and peccadilloes of those who are not, as a matter of fact, imitating God's nature very faithfully.

It is only if we understand this true nature of church government that we see clearly the differences between it and democracy on the one hand or any form of imposed government on the other. The ideal or typical form of church government is, I believe, synodical government, but in case there should be any of you who are historians I had better at once confess that the historians are generally agreed that this ideal or typical form of church government has very rarely been actually realized. But I think that there has always been an awareness, however far the Church has deviated, in whatever direction, that what it was deviating from was synodical government.

I want to illustrate what I believe to be the essential of synodical government, actually outside the sphere of the government of the Church, because of this historical difficulty. In my student days I was a member of the Student Christian Movement. I was at one time on the committee in my university, and the following year I was president, and the year after that I was again on the committee. I don't remember a vote being taken in that committee in those three years. This didn't mean that we didn't take decisions. It meant that we argued through every question until we were agreed, and then the decision probably took the form of the president saying: "Well, I think this sums up what we've been saying, and you will do this, and you will do that . . ." You might describe that as the president giving orders; they weren't orders, because they came out of discussion—and agreement. He was more like the captain of a team than a ruler or a governor.

I wish to deal first with the "sacred synod" of the diocese: let me explain that word "sacred", because people do talk such nonsense about it; the "sacred synod" is the synod of "sacred" people, that is to say of the clergy; they are called "sacred" because they are set apart, which is what the word "sacred" means, and let us not be frightened of it; we are, please God, set apart for our job, and we ought to be.

The sacred synod of a diocese consists, essentially, of the bishop (who of course ought to be elected, and the laity ought to have a decisive voice in that election), surrounded by his clergy, and it is essential to the ideal form that all the clergy should be in the synod. Here at once we get a point that ought to be dealt with in England—that this is quite impracticable in this diocese, the Diocese of London, or several of the others, because the diocese is far too big. One of the reforms which I think is a crying necessity is that we should have smaller dioceses, where all the clergy can be in the sacred synod, and, incidentally, the bishop can know them. Just to show that I am not being wildly unrealistic and impractical, in the interim stage, before we get that necessary reform, the thing to do is for the diocesan synod to meet in sections, and I am happy to see that the Diocese of London has already acted on this suggestion in our report, and has met in sections.

What happens at a synod is that discussion takes place, and in the end the bishop decides in the light of what has been said: not a democratic proceeding at all. But it is rather important to realize that the bishop *never really acts as a bishop until he has listened to his advisers*. And supposing that, when he announces what he believes the decision of the Church to be, some of his advisers think he is wrong, it is quite right for them to say so. The decision still remains his, but he must always listen to his advisers. Now this is something which is quite unlike, as far as I know, any other form of government, but is rather like what I was describing on the committee of the S.C.M. in my student days.

I have left the laity out till this point: I am now going to bring them in, and the heading of my next section is "The Laity and the Holy Spirit". The Holy Spirit, please God, is "in" all the time, when you are talking about church government, but you can't even talk about the laity and their place in church government without bringing the Holy Spirit in.

I ought to insert a point here, because it is a thing which is frequently misunderstood. There has been, in the Western church certainly, a type of phraseology which has divided the church into the teaching section and the learning section, and of course the laity are included in the learning section. *En passant* it is probably important to note that for teachers to teach it is essential that there should be somebody there for them to teach, and therefore the laity are essential. There is another little point which I think is rather important. I don't think the phrase has ever been "The governing church and the governed church". To return to the question of the teaching and learning church: in Anglican circles this distinction has usually been taken to mean that the "teaching church" is the bishops and clergy, and the "learning church" is the laity. In the Church of Rome the "teaching church" is just the bishops, and the "learning church" is the rest of the clergy and the laity. But in that context, of course, the bishop can only do his job as a teacher after he has consulted his presbyters. The presbyters cannot begin to advise without having listened first to the theologians; in the ranks of the theologians there may be some people who by their weight of learning carry very great influence, and there is no reason why some of them should not be lay people. In the Eastern Orthodox Church a great many of the theological teachers are, as a matter of fact, lay people, and although when it comes to government, in the sense of the body that makes decisions, there are no lay people there at all, it would be quite wrong to say that lay people have no influence, because the majority of the theologians are in fact laymen. So that even when this kind of terminology is used it doesn't, if it is properly used, represent a hard division.

What I think is the essential point—I have been hinting at this all the way through—the essential point is unanimity. The Church is the Body of Christ, filled by His spirit, and though He calls different people to different functions within it, it is the whole body, the whole Laos, the People of God, that He inspires and guides. Now that whole body, the Laos, includes bishops, priests, deacons and lay people, and the laity are, of course, an essential part. But do notice that it is not just *representative* lay people that are an essential part of it. It is the whole laity that is essential.

The bishop represents the whole Church to his diocese, and his diocese to the whole Church. When he is fulfilling the latter function, when he is representing the diocese to the whole Church, he may be meeting with his fellow bishops. There are some bishops doing this in Rome at present [1962]. I hope they all remember that this is what they are doing—some of them certainly do, but I rather suspect that there are others who don't. It can happen, you see, when a bishop is functioning in that way, that he doesn't as a matter of fact represent the whole of his diocese particularly well, and then you may get the situation arising where you have a conference or council of bishops which produces some decision which, when they return to their dioceses, the Church repudiates. This happened, in a very famous instance, at the Council of Florence when the issue—one very topical for our age—was Christian unity. They decided on a form of Christian unity to heal the schism between East and West, and when they got back to their dioceses, the dioceses said "no". I think, as a matter of fact, the way that the council was conducted, the kind of arguments and pressures that were involved, were not such as were wholly inspired by the Holy Spirit, and it probably was the guidance of the Holy Spirit in the Church at large which said that "no". The point here is that the essential part of the laity in government is played by all the laity through their obedience to the guidance of the Holy Spirit.

There is a tendency in the discussion of this subject—it came up again and again in our synodical government committee—to equate the clergy with the representative laity, as though it were the representative laity that were essential, rather than the laity as a whole. The laity will, please God, expect the apostolic message to come to them from Christ through the apostolic ministry,

the men sent by Him. But these "men sent", despite that tremendous responsibility, are still men, and they are fallen men.
And those to whom they are sent—the laity—are themselves
part of the spirit-filled body. But if, in the process of the message
being sent, part of it is twisted or falsified, or got just plain wrong,
it may cause an abscess. But the body will extrude what is wrong
—the body of the Church—just as the human body extrudes
dirt from a wound, and this is an essential part of the responsibility of the laity.

I now come on to my next heading: "Representatives of the
Laity in the Government of the Church"—this is what I think I
was probably expected to talk about! The bishop represents the
whole Church to the diocese, and the diocese to the whole
Church. But fairly early in church history it was found convenient, and desirable, that when he was exercising this second
function of representing the whole diocese to the Church he
should take with him clerical advisers. This of course was no
substitute for the unanimous agreement of the clergy of the
diocese, but if he took with him representative clergy they could
make a shrewd guess as to what the unanimous opinion was
likely to be. This is really why we have chaps like me to be with
the bishops in their job at the centre.

Now if it is a good idea to have representative clergy at
national, or provincial, level to provide a shrewd forecast of the
necessary unanimous voice of all the clergy at diocesan level,
then it seems an equally good idea to have representative lay
people at diocesan level to provide a shrewd forecast of the
necessary unanimous voice of all the people in all the parishes. I
therefore think that diocesan synods, in which all the clergy are
included, and of a necessary size to make this possible, are essential, and that until new dioceses are made we should if necessary
meet in sections to provide this. I also think that, in view of what
I have just said, there should be lay people associated with them,
not necessarily to be there to discuss all questions—I think there
are some things which the clergy should discuss on their own—
but for a great majority of questions. I believe that representative

D

laity at diocesan level are vastly more important than anything that happens at the national level, and for the very points
that Peter Whiteley has made. Lay representatives at diocesan
level are closer to the people, and you are more likely to get
there the man who is working in an office, or a shop, or a factory.
Incidentally, would it perhaps help in the meantime if the laity
were able to elect a clergyman to represent them at the centre if
they wanted to? I am not at all certain if, in some cases, for
instance an industrial chaplain might not represent the laity
better than somebody who is, say, seventy-five, and whose last
contact with industry was twenty or thirty years ago.

I believe that all really important matters ought to be referred
to the dioceses. Take, for example, the revision of the prayer
book. I would like to see, on this point, a very wide freedom for
experiment, in order to give the experts some practical material
on which to work, so that their stuff doesn't stink of the lamp,
as it so frequently does. I would allow very wide experiment,
but before anyone could change "The Book"—the Book of
Common Prayer, I would want it to have been down to the
dioceses and accepted by them with overwhelming majorities in
each case, and I wouldn't mind how long it took to reach that
result; it would be worth it. Now, let me say a word or two
about what I would like to see happen at the local level.

The Diocese; Let us have a synod consisting of the bishop, and
shall we say fifty clergy—I don't think we can do with much
more than that; but this would involve a fairly radical dealing
with our diocesan boundaries—and fifty laity associated with
them. Scrap the diocesan conference—I don't think anyone
would very much mind. Have, as Peter Whiteley suggested, a
diocesan council to do the day-to-day work, on which there
would be both clergy and laity. This should take the place of
what there is at the present moment. Few people realize that at
the present time the Church of England is governed not by
synodical government, but by parliamentary government on
one level, and by prelatical government on the other. There is
the bishop, himself state-appointed, entirely surrounded either

by other state-appointed people or by people of his own choice. It is not only that he doesn't consult the *laity* or their elected representatives, he never comes within shouting distance of consulting the elected representatives of the *clergy*. I don't know any diocese in which the Proctors in Convocation really have very much say in how the diocese is run. They are the only elected representatives of the clergy. So let us have a diocese with a bishop, fifty clergy and fifty laity in the diocesan synod, and a proper diocesan council.

The Parish; the Parochial Church Council? I think scrap it— have the old vestry of five or six people. They could do most of the job in half the time and twice as efficiently. When you really need the whole parish there, well, why not have the whole parish? Have a church meeting, and have them all there; from time to time this would be a very good thing to do.

I think—and this is a revolutionary suggestion—that I would like to see the Ruridecanal Conference revivified. As things are I have never seen any use at all in any ruridecanal conference that I have attended—apart from the ones that I have addressed myself (obviously they had some point)—but I can't really see why they should remain useless. If you reduced your parochial church council to the level of a vestry of about five people and you had, say, a dozen clergy and sixty lay people in a ruridecanal conference, that would be a workable kind of party. Really big issues I would send down from the diocesan synod to the ruridecanal conference for discussion, instead of having people like me to go and talk to them. If you want to have somebody like me coming to talk to people on a special subject, arrange a meeting for the purpose. But why have a body which must meet twice a year for this purpose? I would like to see the Ruridecanal Conference a body which meets to *work* on the big issues, either local schemes and plans, or the great issues of church government.

I would like to see church government constructed in that kind of way, so that there is real discussion of all the big questions, right from the top to the bottom, and linked up with the parish.

I said a minute or two ago that I thought what I was really expected to talk about was "representative laity in the *central* government of the Church". Since the whole principle of church government is unanimity—government by agreement—I believe that it is sheer waste of time to produce machinery which will turn out rapid decisions at the centre. We are not doing that actually *very* rapidly at the moment, but there is rather a pressure that we should. But to produce rapid decisions at "the centre" which result in discontent and disagreement at the real centres, which are the parishes and the dioceses, is no gain in efficiency or saving of time. You need a centre, of course, to facilitate discussion, but as the ultimate power of agreement lies with the whole, the centre must not even seem to have ultimate power. Otherwise there is the inevitable tendency to press towards an imposed government, and this is a denial of the whole nature of church government. I think that the best practical step here in England, to deal with this problem, is to preserve the provincial government of the Provinces of Canterbury and York. We will still need a national body to thrash things out, but if they have to be accepted when they have been thrashed out, in both Canterbury and York, then what is accepted in two places is more likely to be accepted in all the dioceses.

I have dealt all the way through—I explained why at the beginning—chiefly with what one might describe as the Gospel side of church government rather than the law side; with the reflecting of the nature of God, with worship, and so on. But of course there is the other side, of law, which you have got to have, and I think one can bring in at this level things like financial arrangements. To deal with all this we already have the Church Assembly. It's not bad. There is one other argument in favour of it that I can use that Peter Whiteley hasn't used. After attending it—particularly last week—I feel quite convinced that I have got off years and years and years of purgatory! But, you know, we have got to have some sort of body that will deal with the kind of tiresome legislative business that we were dealing with. I think it could be tidied up. Let me say about the synodical government report that it wasn't part of our terms of reference to try and produce a tidier scheme for the Church Assembly. In the process of our discussions we all said again and again that one of the things which we need is to tidy up the Church Assembly. I think it could be smaller; I think a lot of its work could be done in committee, in grand committee, whereby anyone who wanted to produce an amendment could sit on that committee and make his point there, rather than wasting time in the whole body. But there are some points in the present set-up which are just so infuriating that they drive—I think particularly the laity—to drink.

May I touch on one of them, which Peter Whiteley has already referred to: Canon Law and the laity. He mentioned this point because he thought the laity had now won the point of having the right to consider the canons. Actually there wasn't any resistance to this, and they didn't have to "win" it: it was unanimously granted without any discussion at all. This was a great pity, because if we hadn't thought that this was so obviously right and allowed it to go through without discussion, we might have realized what a futile way of doing it we were in fact imposing upon the Church. Because what happens is that the laity discuss the canons on their own. Perhaps they deal with an intricate question which has taken the clergy a long time to thrash out, and about which in the end they have reached a compromise agreement—a real compromise, because people have accepted it and see the point of it—and then this is sent to the House of Laity without anybody there to explain to them why this conclusion has been reached. Anything stupider would be very difficult to imagine. The laity may destroy the balance of a carefully worked out agreement, suggest something which already had been fully discussed and discarded. The clergy are exasperated. The laity do not take kindly to their suggestion being ignored, and no-one is to blame. The present system is quite impossible.

I said at the beginning that I signed the minority report. The minority report produced a flexible scheme under which all questions of doctrine, liturgy and canons are either introduced and discussed in the Church Assembly with the laity present, and then sent to the Convocations for further discussion and revision before they come back to the Church Assembly, or they are introduced in Convocation and sent to the Church Assembly for discussion and revision. And in either case they must be passed in their final form by the Church Assembly with the laity of course there, before the Convocations say whether in that final form they will accept, reject or defer them. Both sides, both the majority and the minority, think that on the big issues there ought to be reference to the dioceses, and though I don't think that they were committed, either side, to anything quite so detailed as what I think is the way that that should be done, there was a measure of agreement to some sort of reference. There were some of the bishops, however, who thought it would be quite enough to refer such questions to the diocesan conferences as at present constituted. This, I am bound to say, doesn't appeal to me. All that would happen would be that the Bishop, or Canon Somebody, would bring up the point and then it would be put to the vote. I don't think that would do.

The Minority scheme provides that the representative laity should have a full part in discussion and decision. They cannot over-rule the clergy, neither can the clergy over-rule them. In the Majority Report a National Synod would take the place of the present Church Assembly (they'd have the same chaps in it), and would abolish the provinces of Canterbury and York as having ultimate authority. The Convocations would still have the power of discussing certain things which were referred to them, but not of decision. It is a much more difficult scheme than ours to put into effect, because it would involve transferring powers from the Convocations to the new National Synod, and this would be a difficult constitutional problem. It would take at least five years—and I gather the lawyers who have been into it think more likely ten years—to put into effect the Majority scheme. Our scheme could be put into effect in probably six months. This is one reason why I think that possibly our scheme is better. It certainly gives the laity everything they ask for, and I think probably a bit more. But what I would stress as a chief difference between these schemes is that our scheme preserves the provinces of Canterbury and York. This is tied up with what I was saying about unanimity being the essence of church government: I think that with the Majority scheme you will almost inevitably get rule by majority and imposed decisions from a central organization.

I want to do everything I can to stop that. I think the Church has got to opt out of centralization in this sense, in dealing with questions of doctrine and liturgy. It is the consent of the whole Church that matters. I have no quarrel with efficiency and centralization when it concerns things like the Church Information Office and finance, but we need to distinguish very carefully between the two kinds of question, and I hope that the next time this is discussed I shall not be in a minority of one.

Since this speech was delivered the Archbishops' compromise scheme has gone far to meet the minority point of view. Two defects remain. First the cumbersome process of creating the National Synod will take years longer than it would to produce the same result by expanding the existing powers of the Church Assembly. Secondly the name National Synod has a misleading effect. By creating "a new National Synod", which is really a smaller version of the present Church Assembly, the illusion is produced of a major reform in the direction of synodical government, while the first step in establishing true synodical government, by reform at the diocesan level, is left untouched.

6

LAITY TRAINING

by

MARK GIBBS

I WANT TO deal particularly with the training of the laity for
their work in the world, for I don't believe we have really taken
enough to heart what the Bishop of Woolwich has said on the
Ministry and the Laity. I recently wrote an article about the
distortion factor in the Church, which always seems to ensure
that we start by talking about the duty of the Church in the
world—and within ten minutes we are talking about the duty
of the Church in the Church. I will remind you of what Peter
Whiteley said, that all of us accept that the chief vocation of the
laity is in the world. If we do, we have got to think very hard
about training the laity for *that* job.

There are two ways in which we ought to consider this training. Firstly, we have a very large established educational
machinery in the Church. It starts, I suppose, with the instruction
of parents at baptism. It goes on through Sunday School and
Children's Church, attendance at morning worship, confirmation, marriage preparation and so on. It includes enormous quan-
tities of education of different qualities in schools of one kind
or another. It includes a considerable amount of B.B.C. and
I.T.V. time. It includes a whole apparatus of religious instruction.
We may feel that this doesn't achieve very much; but we should
also notice that the political parties would be extremely glad to

have such an apparatus for instruction at their disposal. We have riches in this country, and it is very important that we do not forget this, although I am going to deal a little bit later with new experiments which are extra to all this. If our Church educational machinery were properly used, we should produce lively, holy, worldly laymen; and until we have this general apparatus of religious instruction working better, we shall not get very far. That is why I am very glad indeed that we have Harold Wilson to tell us something about Church of England experiments in this matter.

Now I want to give some illustrations of important experiments which are taking place on the Continent. First of all the lay centres, or, as they are called very often, the Academies.

In German they are called *Evangelische Akademien*—generally translated in English "Evangelical Academies", which is a somewhat off-putting phrase. You get the feeling of a secondary school in Inverness with Dr. Billy Graham as dominie. Now this is unfortunate. The phrase was adopted by Dr. Eberhard Müller, who started the first German Academy at Bad Boll just after the war. He meant it in the old platonic sense of a *centre for discussion;* by no means a centre for instruction where people passively listen to what the schoolmaster says. Eberhard Müller, who was a Student Christian Movement secretary in the 1930's, founded Bad Boll with one assistant; he now has a staff of over a hundred. There are something like forty such centres in Europe now, and a considerable number more in America and overseas which are connected with us.

The second movement I would say a little about is the German *Kirchentag*, or Church Congress Movement. That again is a little forbidding. We think mostly in terms of, perhaps, an Anglo-Catholic Congress or Eucharistic Congress. This is a layman's conference. It is organized every two years. It collects together forty to fifty thousand people, not for one day, but for four or five days' instruction, and it assembles half a million people together at the final service. But neither the buildings which the Academies have in plenty, nor the numbers who come to the

Kirchentag, count tuppence unless the kind of education they offer is satisfactory. It is because they offer a kind of education for the layman *in the world* that I think they are important for us to know something about.

The principles of this lay education are these. The Christian has a duty to try to find the mind of Christ for his job as a Christian man in a worldly environment. In doing this, we must first understand the environment. We must know where we are placed. And in teaching us this God may easily speak to us through secular experts—not necessarily through our friends in the Church, or even through the clergy and the bishops. If we want to understand how Christians must live as second-hand car dealers in East Manchester, or as teachers in a secondary-modern school in Leicester, or as housewives in Stepney, one of the things that we must do is to learn all the new sociological knowledge we now have about life in those areas, and the new psychological knowledge we have about how informal groups operate in those areas. And the mind of Christ will be found in such a group of Christians who come together and study, and who are *committed to that kind of life*. For instance, although I know there is great value in industrial chaplains, I do not believe that industrial chaplains can really settle how Christians ought to behave in a given factory—because they pop in and out. They are not involved; their careers, their wages and their families are not involved in sticking it in that particular factory. The mind of Christ is found by the people who are working in that factory who are committed Christians, whether they are the directors or the tea-boys. And I would say that to a large extent the pastoral and priestly work of the Church in that factory must be found in those people; in their human relationships with each other and with their neighbours, for whom Christ died. There is a certain autonomy given to lay people in their work, in their business, in their neighbourhood, in their street.

I will give you some examples of this. The Academy at Hamburg has been very concerned for eight or nine years about the problems of delinquency, and of the police and of the port life in

Hamburg. What they have done is to set up a study group of Christian policemen and Christian magistrates and Christian probation officers, who have worked together on the problems of their duties in that particular kind of work. They have got the top experts in delinquency in the city of Hamburg to talk to them and argue with them. The first question is "Do they know what they are talking about?" not, "Are they regular church-goers?" The idea is, you see, that the Christians should first *listen, listen;* show that they are willing to learn and to listen. The Bishop of Woolwich has mentioned Dr. Peter Berger's book, *The Noise of Solemn Assemblies.*[1] Dr. Berger has had a group of engineers at Hartford, Connecticut, who are themselves working out the ethical problems of having to design rather shoddy things—because they get obsolete quickly.

In the centre at Boldern near Zurich there has been a group of probation officers, some Christians, some not Christians, but all equally concerned with what is happening to the people in their charge. At Tutzing Academy in Bavaria, a group has had Strauss and other leading Bavarian politicians to talk to them about the realities of party politics. For neither the clergy nor the teachers can talk effectively about the compromises necessary to survive in West German politics: this is a job for those Christians who are *involved* in political life.

Another example (to show all this is not just for highbrow types): at Montreat, in North Carolina, they have had a week-end course for hairdressers and barbers. Because it is hairdressers and barbers who often hear the personal problems of their clients, as a clergyman will not hear them.

So firstly, get a group together and listen. And secondly, talk with them—without trying to process them. Talk with the ninety per cent non-church-goers honestly, without feeling, "We'll get their scalps and claim them for the Lord pretty soon now." Someone said at one of the German Academies, "I don't mind coming here: they don't try and get at you." Someone said to me in Sweden a week ago at a lay centre called Rättvik,

[1] See above, p. 20.

"Eighty per cent of the people at this centre are not, in fact, regular church members. They come back time and again. For here there is no polite blackmail." But I could tell you of a centre in the States where they pretend to be as open as heaven, and in fact they are as unscrupulous as hell. They make sure that the right line is always said at the end. Their assumption is that the Church knows all the answers.

Sometimes God talks to us, you see, through non-churchy people, just because we don't know the answers.

I could tell you about another centre near Boston, where they have had together Roman Catholics and Methodists and Protestants, where they all feel *that they are at ease*, because the Church is prepared to listen, because the Church is prepared to discuss, because the Church is prepared to show something of the patience of the Lord Himself in dealing with modern people.

Thirdly, I believe that the principle on which much of this lay training should take place is ecumenical. I am myself a fairly loyal Anglican, a diocesan lay reader and all the rest of it; but I believe that when it comes to teaching about the problems of doctors or dentists, of bakers or butchers, then you don't really want a separate association of Anglican bakers or of Presbyterian dentists. In fact, this should be one of the good ways in which we may quite legitimately work together.

Fourthly, I would suggest that it is not merely a matter of meeting together to discuss, and to argue and to try out what is the Lord's will in our given job and our given area. We shall probably find we need more than a discussion group. We shall need to have some kind of a fellowship together. I believe that the parish clergy have to learn here a principle of dual loyalty, or, if you like, of multiple sovereignty. That is, our loyalty is not merely to our parish, nor even to our Church of England. We are entitled in addition—not instead but in addition—to hold membership of another group. A group perhaps like the Servants of Christ the King; a group perhaps like the Iona Community (of which I am proud to be an associate), like the Sigtuna Centre in Sweden, like the friends at Five Oaks in Ontario, a group centred on a place which is in a way an "extra" spiritual home. Because if we are tough enough to believe in the parish system, and go not to the nicest church we can find but to the church locally which needs us, then in that case we shall need sometimes to argue out our faith together somewhere else—often you can't do it in the parish, because there won't be enough people in your occupation anyway. And we may need, too, to have some kind of spiritual counselling outside the parish.

It is very interesting that almost every one of these centres (which often started in a very worldly way with very worldly people) is now faced with the same problem: what do we do when they wish to worship with us: when they wish to come back to us: when they wish to find in us, in fact, something of a spiritual home?

At Rättvik, for instance, they are building a retreat house. They have been under strong criticism from some members of the Church of Sweden for doing this. But it is not the sort of retreat house where you sit at an impossible desk and submit to being lectured. It is a worldly retreat house. It is centrally heated for one thing, and it is built in a decent modern style. Three-quarters of it is for silence; and there are double doors so that you can really be silent. It has rooms for writers to finish their books. A room for an engineer to work on his drawings. A room where you can have a conducted retreat, and a lot of places where you can just be quiet. And the other side of the house (which is open so that you can always go from one end to the other) is a place where you can play records, where you can talk, where you can plan a walk. And this house is being built not because regular church members of the Church of Sweden want it, but because the eighty per cent of the people who go to that centre from the world hunger for it. And I think it is fair to say that if we could find *that* kind of retreat house, a good many people who are not perhaps accustomed to the traditional kind of retreat would be prepared to go there—to what might be called more sensibly an "Advance House".

The same principles come up in the Kirchentag, and in some

of the other smaller church congresses which have been started in Scotland, France, Switzerland and Norway. The Kirchentag is, of course, a great demonstration, and as such it is, I am glad to say, efficiently organized. I agree very much with Peter Whiteley that efficiency is a very important thing for the Church to show in the world which doesn't like muddle. But what is more important is: who comes? and: what is taught?

Who comes? Sometimes only about half of them are regular church-goers. A great many are people from the district who are interested in the faith, but are not in fact connected with any parish. And what is taught? All the most difficult problems of being a Christian in Germany today. We have had, for instance, endless political rows at the Kirchentag, and I am very glad. What on earth would be the use of a German church congress which did not talk about East and West, the lost provinces, the past—and the future? There has been a lot of controversy about this (in fact we are now a suspect organization in Eastern Germany), but what would be the use? We were also under great criticism because we went once to Leipzig in the Soviet Zone. But what would be the use if we did not? For German Christians must face the questions of being Germans—in a divided Germany.

Do you know what the most important theme was at the Berlin Kirchentag last time, in 1961? It was not in fact the Wall. The Congress took place a fortnight before the Wall was built. In the year of the Eichmann Trial, a main theme of the Kirchentag was *Jews and Christians*. We had the Rabbi of Berlin, and the librarian of the Wiener Library here in London (which has perhaps the best catalogue of Nazi atrocities in the world), to come and speak. There was, of course, a certain amount of controversy and heart-searching about this; but it did mean that German Christians faced together some of their fundamental responsibilities.

In 1963 we are going to Dortmund, in the Ruhr; and the problems we face will be those of the Church in the Big City. Michael Jackson wrote recently that the Bible begins in a garden and ends in a city. The Christians start in the city and move out to the suburbs and the gardens. We have got to learn today how to live in an urban environment; and this I think will be a very good thing for a Kirchentag to study.

Now, what can we do in Britain about this? I am glad that Mr. Leslie Paul refers to some of the centres we have in Britain. There is Moor Park: there are diocesan centres like Wychcroft, and particularly, of course, there is William Temple College. I am sure Lord March would like me to say that if we could ever get more people to conferences like the ones they have there, we could soon have an articulate laity, and one knowing in particular its job in the industrial world.

We have also a good deal of knowledge about diocesan training. Harold Wilson will be telling us about that. We need, it seems to me, careful thought as to how we use the more traditional kind of religious education in lay training. What is appalling, you know, is the quality of the little confirmation books that are still given out. What is appalling is the kind of divinity you still hear taught in church or in state schools. And if the whole apparatus of religious education up to the age of eighteen makes you think that the Church is to be run by the clergy as a club for old folk, you cannot easily reverse that impression suddenly by one or two shock conferences. I would hope that as we go to a bigger Keble lay conference we look very carefully at this, because (as in so much of English education) I fear we are stuck in a position which is not very relevant now to the twentieth century.

7

LAITY AND CLERGY: A TECHNIQUE FOR CO-OPERATION

by

HAROLD   WILSON

I WANT TO define my terms. When I speak about "ministry" I
mean the ministry of our Lord himself, which is shared by all of
the people of God: the ministry of this great High Priest, who
in addition to being a Priest is a Deacon—a permanent Deacon;
and I think we would do well to remember this, that in the great
High Priesthood of our Lord there is always this permanent
ministry of serving the world, and it is to this permanent diaconate that I think all of us are called. This includes the whole of
the people of God: some are called to be evangelists, some
preachers, some teachers, some engine drivers, some bus drivers,
and so on, and this ministry of our Lord is the important thing
in which all of us have a share. This means, then, that when I
talk about "laity" I don't mean the people who wear collars and
ties as distinct from dog collars: I mean both parsons and laymen,
the whole of the people of God sharing in this ministry of service
to God's world.

It is important when we have laity conferences—and I mean
conferences of people who are not ordained to Holy Orders—
that we do not throw the clergy entirely out of the window. I
know that in some cases it is a very good idea, but nevertheless
the Church does hold both categories. There are always more

non-ordained people than ordained, and the numbers of clergy available for the vastly increasing population are very few indeed. This means that if we are to take advantage of all the new opportunities for service in the world, we have got to have a policy which is really economic. You have been hearing about these tremendous resources which we have already within our Christian congregations, and you will be just as appalled as I am that so many of these resources go to waste; so our first task is to be economic in the use of what we have. This means careful planning, and from the Church of England point of view I accept all that Mark Gibbs has said about the fact that the education of the laity can only be done in the last resort ecumenically. But we have to begin somewhere, and we meet as a group of Anglicans, and we have plenty of work to do on our own particular pitch in order to equip us to go the next step and do ecumenical work. I don't think that it is a next step, it is one that we ought to be doing at the same time, but nevertheless I am going to limit myself now to talking about the Anglican approach.

In the Church of England we have forty-three dioceses, and every diocese is a law unto itself; each is as independent as a Congregational chapel. What the bishop says there goes, and unless the bishop is behind any plan it is destined to fail in the long run; so our first task is to look at the diocese and to try to design an approach which will fit that particular diocese, because there can never be just one scheme for training. The circumstances in Cornwall are vastly different from Carlisle, and what works in Halton in Leeds does not necessarily work in Liverpool. So we have to begin to look at the situation and make some kind of survey before we begin, and our general approach is first of all to the bishop of a diocese who is asked to call together a group of his clergy and laity.

Sometimes this has to be done in two sections, for the simple reason that it is difficult to get clergy and lay people together at the same time. But these groups come together, and are usually specially selected: one group may be from a number of parishes who have done Christian stewardship and wish to find out how best to follow it up: another group may be like the East Manchester group of clergy who are all working in the same situation, which has the same industrial and sociological problems; or it may be a group of priests who are all working in housing estates. So these clergy come together round the bishop, and this is essential. It demonstrates the overall pastoral care of the bishop who, every time he institutes a priest to a living, says "This is my charge and yours."

In this consultation all that we do is to discuss the issues of their particular situation, and decide which of these issues we can tackle at the present time. Again, being economic, we cannot do everything in one operation: we have to go step by step. I would emphasize the importance of having laymen in this group for the reasons Mark Gibbs has given. It is the barber who knows more about people's problems today, and the parson is no longer the only one who is giving godly counsel and spiritual advice. Since the last war there are a whole lot of new professions of counsellors—hospital almoners, works welfare officers, personnel managers and so on—a whole lot of people who are professionally engaged in giving godly counsel and spiritual advice. This is not a matter for regret; it is a matter for rejoicing, and we who are ordained, and have theological and biblical knowledge, ought to be putting at the disposal of these counsellors all the insights that we can give in order to help them to be more efficient. This is not decreasing the parson's status; it is increasing it, and it is extending the whole ministry.

Having had this consultation and decided on a plan, each parish priest then goes back to his parish and selects a group of laity. I ask for a minimum of five from each parish: sometimes this is not possible, but we know from experience that a group of less than five disintegrates very rapidly, and it has this advantage, that when five people report back to a parish they are not regarded as people with "chips on their shoulders" or "bees in their bonnets". This is a group who are accepted as a group, and they give mutual support and encouragement. Having got five people, this means that from about eight or nine parishes we get a group of between forty and fifty, who are asked to come for three residential week-ends. All time is God's, and therefore we make no excuse about making a big demand. If you put a thing at its true value, people will accept it. If you say "Well, perhaps you would come and spend an hour", they say "If it is only important enough to take up an hour it cannot be very important." But three week-ends spread over the whole period of one year or eighteen months is the first demand that we make. This means that we are being very selective in our recruitment. We have to be, because we do not have any resources to waste, and so we have to pick our very best people.

Having got these people to come to a group, we have a first laity conference, and I will describe the working of that first week-end later. We start where the people are, and I will give you an indication of how we do this; but having got the group of people together, the first week-end is primarily a listening week-end. We don't try to suggest any answers, because in a new group invariably the lay people tend to ask the kind of questions which they think the parson would like them to ask, and we are not interested in those. We have to spend some time letting the group become alive and sensitive to each other, in order that they can have the freedom to ask real questions and to observe carefully.

Obviously not much else can be done at the first week-end, Friday night until Sunday night, and so what we do is to plan the agenda for the next meeting. The second laity conference deals with all the material, or such material as we can, that is produced at the first week-end. Then the third week-end, which is the last, is the one of training for specific tasks, because at the end of the second week-end the people more or less decide on what their groups ought to be doing in this business of engaging in the work. The last week-end is spent deciding on aids and helps required in order to equip that group of people for their particular ministry, wherever it happens to be.

You can guess that when forty people have met together for three week-ends they have got to the stage where they want an annual dinner and a club tie, they become so integrated! This is discouraged; we are not anxious to build up a new pharisaical group in the Church of England—"Lo! we are the trained laity" —so we disband this group after three week-ends, because the ministry of lay people is not a closed group, it is out in the world and back in the parish. We who are professionally engaged in the teaching work of the Church would be doing the Church a great dis-service if we were pulling people out of their own situation. Our task is to service the on-going work of the mission of the Church. A laity conference or training week-end is only one operation in order to improve the on-going work.

Very often we have to do much more than this because several things crop up. Some people may have got a new glimpse of the treasures of the Bible, and may wish to do more Bible study. But forty people won't want to do this, and we can't gather forty people from a large district together with any regularity, so in the meantime we establish local workshops. I think it is better to establish a workshop which has a specific task and a limited length of time than to try to get people to join a society which goes on for ever, and so from this group of forty we might get a dozen people who want to learn more about the Bible; and we start a Bible workshop. There may be some people who have heard about the ecumenical movement, and want to know more about it, so we start an ecumenical workshop. There may be several people who are really interested in children's work, or youth work, and so we start a workshop about whichever subjects are dominant.

This is where the teaching mission of the whole Church comes in, because the staff from London or the diocese cannot possibly cope with all this work, and this is where we begin to use our resources from the local clergy. Among the clergy there are lots of men who have many gifts to offer, and who are just stagnating because they are hardly ever used. So then, after each week-end we always have another consultation for the clergy who have sent the parishioners, in order to do a parallel training operation, because it is a twofold task working with the clergy and laity. It is this dialogue which goes on all the time that helps the clergy to work more effectively with the groups of lay people in the parish, and these clergy service these particular groups.

Now, if this is a deanery or an area group of clergy, we have evolved a co-operative ministry in quite a natural way without all the worries of freehold and of legal squabbles. We have helped a deanery or an area unit to become in a real sense a team ministry, because each man with his gifts is servicing not only his own parish, but a much bigger group. These workshop groups go on sometimes for a short period, sometimes for a longer one.

Alongside this diocesan picture we have to do two other important things. The first we do from the Board of Education, because it can only be done nationally. We establish what we call training institutes. This on-going work of the Church in the diocese must be self-supporting. We cannot always bring in speakers and leaders from all over the country. We have to build up a team of people in every diocese, both clergy and lay people, who will make it their specific responsibility to learn the skills required to do this kind of teaching operation, and gradually we are building up such teams of people. In each diocese we then establish a teaching unit which is at a more advanced level, where we deal regularly with teaching skills, looking at the sociological issues, and making surveys of districts and so on, in order that every diocese has a mobile column of clergy and laity who can give service where they are required.

One of the urgent needs at the moment is to have a large group of lay people who will give some time to learning such skills, so that we can service the tremendous enthusiasm which has been thrown up as a result of the Christian stewardship campaigns. "How do we deal with time and talents?" we ask. As you know, this cannot be done in an eight-day campaign, but what can be done is to have a corps of laymen who will spend six weeks or so visiting one particular parish in a diocese in order to help them and put them on a working basis for Christian education in that parish. We have a team in the London diocese which is just beginning to be useful in this sense, but we need many more, and this is, I think, a very economic way of using this vast potential which we have in the lay people.

Alongside the training institute for building up diocesan experts (they are not experts, they are only ordinary people, but I always say that an expert is only an ordinary chap away from home) we have national institutes, or you can call them seminars, or conferences, where we draw together selected people from these diocesan groups to look from a deeper level at some of these important issues. One such consultation, led by Hans Rudi Weber from the Department of Laity at the Ecumenical Institute at Bossey, was spent thinking about the theology of laity. We had four Bible schools this year to help clergy and lay people in the technique of Bible study. These were led by Mlle. Suzanne de Dietrich. Next year we are having such a seminar about the deployment of all these trained people in the on-going life of the parish, and also this year we have had two very intensive schools learning about group studies and techniques of leadership. I have a bee in my bonnet about the importance of working with groups, observing them, and finding out how groups can be helped to give a maximum contribution, and how the individual can come to life within a group and so on. Well, that more or less is the kind of procedure that we adopt.

How, then, do we begin? Lay people might be anything, and if I arrive in Birmingham next week, as I intend to do, at a conference house, I shall be presented with forty lay people. Most of them I shall not have seen before, but in this group I might have bus drivers, steel workers, a married couple, a housewife, a schoolteacher, a solicitor and maybe a doctor: all with different levels of education, all with different interests, different aptitudes. What is the level at which we direct our teaching?

Well, we have to find this out and we begin by sending them off into groups and giving them four headings: International, National, Vocational and Ecclesiastical. We say "Right, go off to groups straight away, and talk for an hour, and then come back and decide what one question your group would most like to ask under these four headings." You can guess the sort of questions which are asked, e.g. under International we might have Cuba; the H-bomb; Colour, etc. On the National level we might have the Election, or the Spy Case—and you can think of many others. On the Vocational level, in Birmingham at the moment it would almost certainly be juvenile employment. If it were a group of schoolteachers it might well be the 11-plus examination. If it were a group of miners it might be rates of pay for Sunday work. If we were at Dagenham, you know what the question would be there. Ecclesiastical: this is the really interesting bit, because under Ecclesiastical we get anything from the fact that the vicar always chooses hymns that we can't sing, to the filioque clause, and this more or less gives a measure of the general understanding. It is important, if people go to church and can't sing the hymns, that this subject be aired, and the vicar must learn that he must choose hymns which are suitable, and organists too, if they are in the habit of playing the hymns too quickly, and so on.

Having got all this material, what on earth do we do with it? We do not give them thirty-six lectures on the Creed, but we might begin with the first bit of the Creed, "I believe in God...", and this is a very elementary approach. What do we believe about God? He is a Father; He is a Son, and He is Holy Ghost. What does the Father do? Creator of heaven and earth—oh yes, we've said that twice today in the Creed. What does the Son do? He redeems. What does the Holy Ghost do? He sanctifies. What is that? Disinfecting? We reduce it to kindergarten terms— making holy. And so we take the first bit of the Creed about God and for the rest of the week-end we do an exercise in relation-ships: How does God the Father Creator come into Cuba? How does God the Son redeem in Cuba? How is the Holy Ghost making it holy? What has God the Father got to do with silly hymns? How is the Son redeeming them? How are they being made holy? No doubt you are asking, "How do we do this?" There are many methods of teaching, but basically all our theo-logy must be relevant, otherwise it is of no use.

There are three basic needs which crop up under all these

questions in every group of clergy and lay people. These needs
are:

i. First of all the layman wants to know what is the nature of
biblical authority today. How do we help Christians to think
biblically? They have heard all this about Dead Sea Scrolls and
Gospels of Thomas until the poor things don't know where they
are. They don't know whether they can use the Bible as a kind of
Old Moore's almanac, or whether they have to throw it away.

ii. The second point is, how do we relate the Christian faith to
daily life? What is the Christian faith and what are the grounds
for this belief? We have to help lay people to think biblically,
we have to help people to have faith and be able to see its relevance in this life of the world in which they are engaged and in
which they are performing their diaconate every day of their
lives.

iii. The third need is to see the relevance of the worshipping
community. We talk such a lot about services and going to
church, and this is important; the eucharist is the heart of all that
we believe. What then is the relation of this worshipping community to life in the world? Why is Sunday divorced from all
the other days? Under this heading we have to discuss the personal life of the Christian—what is the pattern of lay spirituality
in this world? Here again, I am with Mark Gibbs when he pours
scorn on all those confirmation manuals. You know—twelve
points that a Christian ought to do; you have to meditate for
forty minutes every day, and say not only Mattins and Evensong,
but the canonical Hours as well. This is all right for parsons, you
say, it's what they are paid for: they have the time. It is easy when
all you have to do is to walk into church and that's just as natural
as getting on a bus to go to the factory. But for a layman who
lives in a council house and has four children, two of whom have
been screaming all night with toothache, and a wife who is not
very well and he has to make the breakfast and get the kids off to
school and then catch the train—he just hasn't the time for twenty
minutes' Bible reading; he barely has time for two minutes'
quiet.

So with these groups—and every different group has a different approach to this—we have to help them to think out a new pattern of spirituality, because this is important, and one of the things which often happens is that the second week-end is spent doing spiritual exercises. Not along the old traditional pattern of a retreat, but very often a much more informal approach to spirituality, when the book which we read is not so much the Bible as a book like Alan Harrington's novel *Life in the 'Crystal Palace'*,[1] which tells all about the pressures in modern industry. Alternatively we might even take the book mentioned already, *The Noise of Solemn Assemblies*.[2] But there are many relevant novels, and quite a lot of plays which have been running in the theatres recently, which demonstrate more theological insights than many of the sermons which we clergy produce. So let us use the novelists, and let us use the playwrights, in fact anybody who is going to contribute towards solving some of these issues, and which can so form the basis of our exercise in lay spirituality.

Now what is the actual method of getting down to brass tacks and looking at this? How do we relate the Bible to everyday life? You may have read the excellent book by Paul Tillich called *The Courage to Be*.[3] It is now in a paperback, and very well worth your struggling with it. It is not the easiest book to read, but he gives as his diagnosis of all the spiritual neurosis of the world, three basic reasons. First of all there is this tremendous fear of death, secondly there is the feeling of guilt, and thirdly there is this feeling of meaninglessness. Now, you see, it's easy to stand up in a pulpit and say "Ah yes, these three needs. Well, obviously we have the answers. The answer to death is resurrection: the answer to guilt is forgiveness: the answer to meaninglessness is all that we teach about the Kingdom." Here is the synopsis of a good sermon, you say, "Q.E.D."! As you well know, it is not as easy as that; it is this task of relating what we know are the

[1] Cape, 1960.
[2] See above, p. 20
[3] Nisbet, 1952.

resources of our faith to the real situation we face which is the difficulty.

These are the lines which suggest to us this mission of Christian education, and these lines are never quite as direct as that. They are much more likely to be wiggly lines. How on earth does the Creator come into that? you say, and with all kinds of difficulties and red herrings coming into the discussion all the time, it is not easy to show this direct line. But this line of relationship makes our task of training a group of lay people one of the most fascinating in the whole life and work of the Church today. For example, take this fear of death. Resurrection is the plank of our Christian belief; if it is not true, we are wasting our time. Yet, if I said I was going to give a lecture on "the resurrection" tonight, how many of you would stay over and listen to it? One or two of you may stay out of politeness, or because you have nothing else to do, but on the whole I suspect most of you would be much more interested in catching your trains and going home. I think this is true of a parish. People are not particularly interested in this, particularly young people; and yet here is the resurrection, the cardinal point of faith.

So of course we forget all about lectures, and what we do in our groups is to give out a sheet of paper with a case history, and this case history might have been taken from almost any house in Coronation Street, or from the Archers, or from Mrs. Dale's Diary: incidents which are real people, not fictitious cases, and this way it is absolutely essential to have your barbers and your hospital almoners and your solicitors in your consultation group. They are the people who know what these case histories are, not the parson, because the parson is that one degree removed from the situation. If he is a sensitive parson, and I hope he is, he will have his ear glued to what these people are saying.

So the groups are given a case history like this. Barry Briggs, a seventeen year old boy, very popular, always willing to lend his gramophone records to the Youth Club, has a number of girl friends. He has as much impudence as he ought to have at seventeen: everybody likes him, in fact he is the secretary of the local Youth Club. He is also quite a bright lad; he got himself a scholarship to the local grammar school, and just recently he has been given a county award in order to go up to Oxbridge the following October. Being an efficient club secretary he has organized a club holiday, and all the group went off on a cycling holiday to the Norfolk Broads, but as they were cycling through Cambridge a huge lorry swerved out of the road, knocking Barry from his bike, killing him instantly. You can imagine that this was a tremendous blow to the club and to the parish, and being an efficient parish with a good deal of fellowship, they were very disturbed and concerned about this. A group of people went to see Mrs. Briggs, Barry's mother, and offered sympathy, but she turned round and said, "I can't believe there's a God, if he'd allow such a thing to happen to a boy like Barry—after all he's done for the church."

I think this is a real situation. What does the group do now? We shall try to approach this question informally. The television has the greatest influence on education today, I think, and so we are going to be script writers. Each group goes off to its corner and devises a ten-minute television programme which begins with this meeting point: the group visit Mrs. Briggs who begins by saying, "I can't believe in God if he'd allow such a thing to happen to a boy like Barry, after all he's done for the church," and the group has to deal with this situation. In other words, how would you relate how God the Father Creator, how God the Son the Redeemer, how God the Holy Ghost is making holy this situation, and unless you know something about the resurrection, this is not possible.

What is the result of this group project? (Incidentally, the one thing you must not do is to say, "Well, we are very sorry, Mrs. Briggs; we will ask the vicar to call." The vicar is away for three weeks at one of those free Butlins holidays!) From the kind of programme which these groups will produce, we shall list a whole lot of needs. Indeed, some people will be completely puzzled and say "We haven't got a clue." Some people will go off along a different track which leads them nowhere, but the important thing that happens is that each group is beginning to ask itself real questions; and once we have got the real questions, we bring in our resource material, and it is at this point that your theologians and your experts of various kinds come in, and may speak directly to the needs of that group. They do not give *all* the answers; if the seventeen things which they think ought to have been included have not appeared, then we will leave on one side these seventeen things, for that group is not yet ready to deal with these. This is why this approach to laity training is a slow one: it is an expensive one in terms of time and personnel and resources. But I think this is a real attempt to meet the requirements of people in our church at a much deeper level, and it is meeting real situations, not artificial ones.

How then do we integrate this discussion? Having probably talked for a bit about some of the issues of Mrs. Briggs and death and resurrection, we can then say, "Well, what resources do we have to meet this need?", and of course we have two important resources which we badly neglect: the Bible and the prayer book. For the Bible we might take a Bible study, and put out a few verses. Don't give them a whole big Bible which looks as black as night and forbidding as its ten commandments. Isolate a few verses which are relevant, and we might take, say, the story of the raising of the widow's son at Nain: a difficult passage certainly, but we don't try to get every ounce of meaning from this particular portion. The group is asked to pick out the verbs in the passage and write them down on a piece of paper. These are explored with the help of a dictionary. It is incredible how an examination of these "doing" words will help us to get to the heart of that Bible material.

Or again, we might pick out three words which we think important. The sort of words which are constantly coming up are those like "reconciliation", "ministry", "service", "disciple", "salvation", "grace", and once we begin to write these words up, it is very important that we should have a dictionary available, and some word-books and commentaries, and allow people to find the answers for themselves. I think this is most important, because of the changing categories of word values. If you take a word you find you get very many different shades of meaning. E.g., the word "society", which we are always using in our dialogue and talks. If you question a number of people about the meaning of this word "society", you get any amount of different interpretations. The young couples who are buying their house will think of the building society. The teenage girl will think of London society—debutantes and so on. The lads will think of secret societies, and your mums will think it is a posh name for the co-op!

This is much the same situation we get with groups of lay people, so first of all we thrash out what the Bible's meaning is, and this way we bring in all the resources that are available: J. B. Phillips' translation, the Rieu Penguin, the New English Bible, Revised Standard Version, and we say, "Look at this passage in all these versions, and see if all the translators have been forced to use this one word, or if they use an alternative one. What does Phillips use here? What does the New English Bible use?" And by looking up these things for ourselves, we are doing a depth approach to this Bible study, and are getting into the feeling of that Bible passage. We are getting into this habit of thinking biblically, and this is much more relevant to the lives of ordinary people than worrying about questions of demythologizing. Then, having done this Bible study, we come together again and say, "Look at the issues which have come up about Mrs. Briggs, and let's look at the discoveries that we have made with our Bible; have any of these discoveries helped us to solve some of our difficulties?" . . . and so on.

This is the way in which we proceed in our dialogue throughout the week-end, and it may mean establishing further workshops.

It is important to integrate the three needs that I mentioned, and having done the Bible study and case history, the way in which we draw this discussion and work into the life of the worshipping community is by giving each group a task. One group might be asked during the day to write down six things—

and always limit the amount of things they have to do—six things for which they can give special thanks, six new learnings. The next group might be asked to write down six things about which we ought to be sorry—penitence; and the next group might be asked to write down the things we ought to be praying for—intercession.

Later at our prayers or at our eucharist the next morning members of each group will stand up before or during the Prayer for the Church, and recite these lists. So the whole of our life in the conference is taken up with all that we offer and all that we receive at the eucharist.

The Board of Education tries also to service the workshops and subsequent training projects. For example, the study outline *Living the Liturgy Together*,[1] which looks at the Holy Communion service and some of the modern problems of parish worship. This is a book designed for use in parish workshops. The first part is a Bible study, the second is a play reading, the third is discussion, the fourth a twenty-questions quiz; and every meeting of the workshop will have a different approach to the material, and certain methods are suggested. Again, I have mentioned group Bible study. We have put together another little manual which has twenty different methods of approaching group Bible study in this informal way.[2] We have sample case histories, which are all real cases, though the names are disguised, produced by the consultative groups of lay people that we meet in the diocese.[3]

This regular consultation and dialogue which goes on between clergy and people in your diocesan team and in your parish team, and from the centre as well, is absolutely essential to the success of the whole venture. In fact success is a word that we dare not use, because there are casualties in this venture. We do lose

[1] *Living the Liturgy Together*, Harold Wilson and Patrick Appleford. Church Information Office, 2/6d.
[2] *Reading the Bible Together*, Harold Wilson. Church Information Office, 2/6d.
[3] Examples of this informal approach to Christian Education adapted for work with young people are given in *The Parish Youth Club*, Harold Wilson, S.P.C.K., 21/-.

people, and we do make a mess of certain things; but this is the life of the Church, and I think that Christian education is not a thing that you can put in a separate category. It is the blood which enlivens the whole mission of the Church, and it is the on-going work of this equipping the saints for the work of the ministry in which we all have a responsibility, and in which we are all needed.